BATTLEFIELD
GHOSTS

To Stacy

BATTLEFIELD GHOSTS

Best Wishes

B. Keith Toney

B. Keith Toney

7-13-2000

Rockbridge Publishing Company
Berryville, Virginia

A *Katherine Tennery* Book

Published by

Rockbridge Publishing Company
an imprint of
· Howell Press, Inc.
1147 River Road, Suite 2
Charlottesville, Va 22901
Telephone: 804-977-4006
http://www.howellpress.com

© 1997 by B. Keith Toney

Cataloging in Publication Information

Toney, B. Keith (Bryan Keith), 1960—
    Battlefield ghosts / B. Keith Toney.
        p.   cm.
    Includes index.
    ISBN 1-883522-17-X
    1. Ghosts—United States. 2. United States—History—Revolution, 1775-1783—Battlefields—Miscellanea. 3. United States—History—Civil War, 1861-1865—Battlefields—Miscellanea. I. Title.
BF1472.U6.T66   1997
133.1'0973—dc21   97-9931
                                                    CIP

Second printing 1998
10 9 8 7 6 5 4 3 2

TABLE OF CONTENTS

For Billy and Katie

Seeing Ghosts

Growing up in the foothills of the western North Carolina mountains, I could not help but be exposed to two things that developed into a life-long love for me: history and good storytelling. That area is rich with Revolutionary and Civil War history, and I often traveled with my father through the tradition-steeped Carolinas, Tennessee, and Kentucky during the summer. No matter how tight his business schedule was, Dad always made time to visit historic sites or stop and let me read the roadside markers. When we were at home, we visited some of my father's favorite Saturday spots when we were in town for a bit of serious loafing and storytelling. I was enthralled with the tales and have been forever grateful for the experience.

As often as not, those Saturday trips also included a stop at the library and/or the local bookstore, where I stocked up on American military history from the Revolutionary War to the Korean War. I think I must have read every book of regional stories and folklore in the McDowell County Library, too. The ones I enjoyed most of all were the ghost stories.

I have to admit that I've never SEEN a ghost, though not from any lack of effort on my part. It just hasn't happened for me yet. That's not to say I haven't had a few weird and spooky experiences. I have, for instance, seen on numerous occasions the Brown Mountain

Lights in North Carolina, which many claim are the spirits of Native Americans or Civil War soldiers—take your pick. And I had the bejeezus scared out of me one memorable day when I was about ten years old. My father and I were touring the battlefield at Chicka-mauga, Georgia, when an uneasy feeling stopped me dead in my tracks. I went back to the car while my dad continued on by himself. At least I think he was by himself.

Today, I am very fortunate to have what I consider the best job in the world. Being an historian, writer and a Licensed Battlefield Guide at Gettysburg National Military Park allows me to combine my loves of history and storytelling. When the idea for this book first surfaced, my immediate reaction was not to do it. I wasn't sure I wanted to become known as a ghost hunter. Then, the more I thought about it, the more I realized that I might be overlooking a great opportunity. What better way to tell the story of some of America's greatest and most important battles than by tying them to a good ghost story?

Many of the stories in this book originated with folks like you, many of whom told me, "I never used to believe in ghosts, but ..." Everyone I interviewed has sworn to the accuracy of their experiences. Some have chosen to remain anonymous, and that request has been honored. Some of the stories have been documented in regional newspapers, and in every case efforts were made to get verification. Just because I haven't seen a ghost doesn't mean they're not there. Many people have seen them, and some of their stories are in this book. I hope you will enjoy them and will share your stories with me for future story collections.

Faugh a Ballagh!

ANTIETAM NATIONAL BATTLEFIELD PARK
SHARPSBURG, MARYLAND

"You aren't going to believe this—I didn't believe it at first. But when those kids told me what they'd heard, I knew something weird was going on."

So began the story of a park ranger at Antietam National Battlefield Park, scene of the bloodiest single day of fighting during the American Civil War. Considering the amount of pain, horror and suffering that occurred on that September day in 1862, if any place were likely to harbor lost and disturbed spirits, Antietam would. And apparently the Irish Brigade, one of the most celebrated units of the war, left behind more than the bodies of their slain comrades.

Robert E. Lee's Confederate Army of Northern Virginia had scored two stunning victories against federal armies in July and August—the Seven Days' Battles around Richmond and the great battle at Second Manassas. It appeared to many in the North that the Confederate juggernaut was unstoppable.

Then Lee took his boldest gamble yet—an invasion of Maryland, which had strong Southern leanings, in search of recruits and supplies. His army began crossing the Potomac River into Maryland on September 3 and by the 9th were concentrated in and around the town of Frederick. Disappointed by the lack of anticipated support from the citizens of Maryland, Lee divided his forces, planning to capture the union stronghold at Harpers Ferry and then reunite his troops for a strike into Pennsylvania. By September 12, the Army of Northern Virginia had left Frederick and was headed even farther into Yankee territory. Lee abandoned the northward movement, however, when he learned that union general George McClellan had obtained a copy of his marching orders. They had been found lying in a field near Frederick, Maryland. How they got there is a mystery yet to be solved.

McClellan, in one of his finest moments as a commander, reorganized the bruised Army of the Potomac and set off in pursuit of Lee. It was a typical McClellan pursuit—slow and deliberate— which enabled Lee to begin moving his troops toward the Potomac River, where he intended to cross back into Virginia. His plans changed again, however, after he surveyed the ground near the small village of Sharpsburg, Maryland, three miles from the river. There he offered battle to McClellan. By September 16 the two armies were positioned on opposite sides of Antietam Creek, which meandered through the rolling farmland.

The fighting began at 5:30 on the morning of the 17th when troops from Major General Joseph ("Fighting Joe") Hooker's Federal I Corps were sent forward against General Thomas J. ("Stonewall") Jackson's Confederates posted in and near a cornfield owned by farmer David Miller. Over the next four and a half hours the fighting progressed in a generally southerly direction, toward the Dunker Church, leaving thousands of dead and wounded from both sides strewn about the blood-soaked fields.

Beginning around 10 a.m., the union division under the command of Brigadier General William French launched an attack against a confederate stronghold near the center of the line. Two rebel brigades under generals Robert Rodes and George B. Anderson were posted in an old farm lane known locally as the Sunken Road. A heavily travelled thoroughfare, it was worn away by use and natural erosion, so much so that a long stretch of the road had sunk several feet below the level of the surrounding fields. By day's end, this natural rifle pit would be known forever more by a new name: Bloody Lane.

French's troops were met by a withering fire from Rodes's Confederates, who were ensconced in the relative safety of the lane. Unable to withstand the terrible blasts of musketry being poured into them, the Federals fell back.

On French's left, Brigadier General Israel Richardson's division had arrived. The decision was made to launch another attack against the confederate center. Richardson chose the most colorful and recognizable brigade under his command to make the first attempt—Brigadier General Thomas Meagher's Irish Brigade.

Meagher, a dashing and controversial Irishman, had recruited a brigade comprising native sons of Erin from his adopted home state of New York. Three regiments—the 63rd, 69th and 88th New York—were formed by the men who had answered Meagher's call to preserve the union of their new homeland. Although the New Yorkers had by this time been reinforced by the 28th Massachusetts Infantry, who were not Irish, the original members of the brigade marched proudly to battle under a large green flag emblazoned with the Celtic harp that symbolized their native land.

Undaunted by the failure of French's men to penetrate the confederate defenses, the Irish Brigade moved forward. A bit farther south along the lane Anderson's battle-tested brigade of Confederates waited patiently. As the Irish Brigade crested the hill, the Confederates opened fire. Within minutes the flag of the 69th New York had fallen three times, the brigade stopped in its tracks by the hellish fire. General Meagher rode to the front of the line and cried out, "Come on, boys, raise the colors and follow me!" Inspired by their commander, the Irish Brigade moved on.

The Confederates heard a chilling cry rise from the ranks of the steadily advancing enemy. Over and over, as if the phrase alone could drive the Confederates out of their stronghold, came the old Gaelic

war chant: "Faugh a ballagh! Faugh a ballagh! Faugh a ballagh!"
Translated loosely, it means, "Clear the way."

Although they were empowered with these ancient words, the
Irish Brigade's advance ground to a halt less than a hundred yards
from the confederate line. From there they traded volleys with the
Confederates until they were nearly out of ammunition, and only
then did they fall back.

Eventually the confederate center gave way, and the Irish Brigade
moved forward once again. As the fighting moved even farther south,
toward the crossing known today as Burnside Bridge, the grisly price
paid by the Irish Brigade for this bloody day's work in service to their
country was tallied: 540 casualties out of the slightly more than 1,000
who entered the fight. More than half of their comrades had fallen.
As mind-boggling as those numbers were, they were but a small part
of the total casualties that day—more than 23,000 killed, wounded,
or missing.

General Lee had narrowly averted disaster at Antietam, and he
was able to slip back across the Potomac to the relative safety of
Virginia to prepare to do battle another day. Before long the Irish
Brigade, along with the rest of the Union army, left the bloodied fields
of Sharpsburg to pursue Lee's army.

Or did they?

According to the park ranger, apparently not all of the Irish
Brigade left. "This happened a few years ago," he told me. "A private
boys' school in Baltimore brings some of their students for a tour of
the battlefield every year. More often than not, I'm the one who takes
them around. We start up on the north end in the morning, work
our way through the cornfield and end up at the Dunker Church. By
then it's lunchtime, we're back by the visitor center, and we break
for lunch.

"After lunch, I take the group into the auditorium and show them
the film [a twenty-minute orientation movie the National Park
Service shows at regular intervals]. Our next stop is Bloody Lane,
where I split the group in two, keeping one group up near the bend
in the lane and sending the other one down to the tower [an

observation tower built near the turn of the century]. I tell the kids to think about the movie they just saw, what they had seen that morning, what they know about what happened where we are now, and how the two fit together. Then we gather back up near the middle and discuss the fight for Bloody Lane. These are 6th, 7th, and 8th graders we're talking about. If there's one of them who knows ahead of time what happened here, I'll eat my hat.

"Anyway, this time when I brought the groups back together, the kids who were down by the tower asked about the singing they'd heard. None of us had heard it. They argued amongst themselves a little, some of them saying it sounded like chanting, others saying it was singing. I had no idea what they were talking about.

"Several of them, whether they described it as singing or chanting, said that it sounded a little like "Jingle Bells"—not the whole song, but just those words, repeated over and over again.

"Well, let me tell you, by that time the hairs on the back of my neck were standing up. I had an idea, but I was almost afraid to find out if I was right. Finally, I asked, 'Fellas, by any chance were you hearing the words "Faugh a ballagh" (pronounced fah-lah-ba-LAH)?' As soon as I said the words, they all started yelling, 'Yes, that's it! Wow, how did you know?'

"Now we're talking about kids here—how in this world were they going to know a Gaelic war cry? I've never had such a weird feeling in my life. These kids had been standing on the spot where the Irish Brigade attacked the Bloody Lane, and they heard the war cry almost 130 years after it happened.

"To this day, the boys who were there ask me if people still hear the Irish Brigade at the lane. There have been other reports of unusual sounds in the area, but has anyone else heard the war cry itself? That's hard to say. And to this day I don't know how it happened."

How, indeed?

Write Antietam National Battlefield Park at P.O. Box 158, Sharpsburg, Maryland 21782, or call (301) 432-5124 for park hours.

The Hound of Gettysburg

GETTYSBURG NATIONAL MILITARY PARK
GETTYSBURG, PENNSYLVANIA

The battlefield at Gettysburg, Pennsylvania, site of the Civil War's largest and bloodiest battle, is filled with ghosts. If all the ghost stories were true, the millions of visitors there wouldn't be able to walk without tripping over some troubled spirit. One story that seems to have some subtance is the Ghost Hound.

In early June of 1863 the Confederate Army of Northern Virginia, led by the incomparable Robert E. Lee, invaded the North, looking for an opportunity to end the war by inflicting a crushing defeat on the Union Army of the Potomac on the Yankees' home turf.

The Confederates roamed freely through the green Pennsylvania countryside gathering much-needed supplies until June 29. That morning, having learned that the Federals were in hot pursuit, Lee began to concentrate his widely scattered army. A look at the map dictated the logical point: the little town of Gettysburg.

The Union army, under the direction of their new commander, Major General George G. Meade, moved northward in search of the Confederates. President Lincoln expected Meade to find Lee and stop him—soon. The general looked at the map and saw that for his army, all roads also led to Gettysburg. Thus was the stage set for a chance meeting that would make history.

On the first day the Confederates drove the union forces through the town back onto high ground south of the village. As the two armies concentrated rapidly through the night, the lines were drawn—the Confederates along Seminary Ridge and the Federals along a hook-shaped series of hills and higher ground known as Cemetery Ridge.

On the second day Lee attacked Meade despite the Union army's strong position and the protests of his senior lieutenant, James Longstreet. Around 4 p.m. the First Corps launched a series of attacks on the south end of the battlefield against the union left. Wave after wave of Confederates threw themselves against such strongholds as Devil's Den, Little Round Top and the Wheatfield.

Near the center of the confederate line and impatiently awaiting his chance to advance was Brigadier General William Barksdale, a fiery Mississippian and former U.S. congressman. Finally the word came, and Barksdale, on horseback, led his brigade forward. They struck the union line at John Sherfy's peach orchard along the Emmitsburg Road, where Major General Daniel Sickles's III Corps had bent the line back at a forty-five-degree angle. The Mississippians smashed through the orchard and continued on, sweeping everything before them back toward Cemetery Ridge.

Somewhere between the farm of Abraham Trostle and the banks of Plum Run, a small stream a few hundred yards below the crest of Cemetery Ridge, Barksdale went down, still at the head of his brigade. Exactly who fired the shot, no one knows, though many surmise that it may have come from the 1st Minnesota Regiment.

In any event, as Barksdale's Mississippians streamed back toward their own lines, their charge having finally spent itself against a new, stronger union line near Plum Run, Barksdale was left behind. Before long a group of federal stretcher-bearers found the fallen general and carried him back to a field hospital established at the farm of Jacob Hummelbaugh near the Taneytown Road. A union surgeon took one look at the chest wound and informed Barksdale that it was mortal; he would not survive. The general lingered on for several hours, but at midnight on July 2, 1863, the fire-eating congressman from Mississippi breathed his last. General Barksdale was buried in the Hummelbaugh farmyard on the third while the battle raged on toward its dramatic conclusion, Pickett's charge.

In the days and weeks that followed the battle of Gettysburg, hundreds came to the little town to search out the fate of loved ones. Many were cautiously hopeful they would find the husband, lover, son or brother lying among the more than 21,000 wounded the two armies had left behind. Others came to undertake the heartbreaking task of carrying their loved one's remains back home for burial. Among the Southerners who made the long trek to Gettysburg was General Barksdale's widow—and herein lies our tale.

Mrs. Barksdale was accompanied on her mournful journey by Barksdale's favorite hunting dog. As the faithful hound was led near the resting place of his master, he broke free, threw himself to the ground near the grave and broke into a plaintive howl. The animal refused to leave the spot while the general's remains were being exhumed and even after the remains were carried away, despite all manner of cajoling by Mrs. Barksdale. All through the night the dog kept watch over the gravesite of his master. The next day, Mrs. Barksdale tried again to lure the dog from his post, and once again she failed. Finally, her heart now doubly broken by the dog's pitiful loyalty, she left for home.

For those who lived in the area, it was difficult not to be aware of the general's loyal and lonely pet, as the dog occasionally let out a heart-wrenching wail that could be heard for a great distance. Despite the best efforts of several concerned parties, the dog refused to take any type of sustenance, rejecting all food and water. Eventually the inevitable happened, and General Barksdale's faithful hound died, still pining for his lost master.

Within a few years, though, a strange tale began circulating among the locals and visitors to Gettysburg. Don't go near the Hummel-baugh farm at midnight on July 2, they warned one another, for you'll experience the most unearthly howl your ears will ever hear.

Barksdale's dog was still there, they claimed, standing guard and awaiting the return of his master.

For several years a number of friends and I positioned ourselves near the Hummelbaugh farm before midnight on that date and awaited the return of the faithful hound. We never saw the hound, yet I'm convinced that the last year I took part in the vigil, I came very close.

The Hummelbaugh farm, like most of the farms and houses on the Gettysburg Battlefield, is owned by the U.S. National Park Service and provides housing for the rangers and other park employees. Less than a hundred yards from the house itself is the park's maintenance building, with only a park road and a few yards of grass separating the two. We would park beside the road between the two buildings and remain there until past midnight, yet the fickle hound never showed up.

On the night that something did happen, the farmhouse was occupied by a park ranger who has since left the park service and returned to her home in the West. The sounds of our conversation caught her attention, and she came to her door and talked with us for a few minutes. Finally, around 12:30 a.m. we gave up and went home.

I went to bed disappointed that once again Barksdale's hound had failed to make an appearance and wondered why we'd never seen him. I had a sneaking suspicion I was missing something, and then it hit me. I was smiling as I finally fell asleep.

The next morning, eager to test my theory, I asked the ranger if by any chance she had still been awake around 1 a.m. She gave me a slightly odd look. "So that was you," she said. "It wasn't funny, and what's more, you could have been hurt or in big trouble if you'd been caught."

I told her I hadn't the faintest idea what she was talking about, that I was merely curious and testing a theory. "Do you mean to tell me that you weren't in the maintenance barn last night?" she asked.

I assured her that I had been home in my own bed at one o'clock and she was free to call my wife to confirm I was telling the truth.

"Well," she admitted, "Something odd did happen. After you guys left, I couldn't get back to sleep right away. I was sitting in the living room when the lights in the maintenance barn came on and then went off a minute later. I didn't think anything of it until they came back on again. I thought the first time that it might have been one of the patrol rangers checking, but I couldn't figure why the lights would have come back on. I went to the window to check. I didn't see anything unusual, but while I stood there watching they went out and then, just a minute or so later, came back on.

"I started to get a little nervous, so I called the patrol ranger on the radio and asked him to come check out the barn. Before he pulled up about three minutes later, the lights did their on-and-off thing twice more.

"When he got there the lights were on, and they stayed on while he walked up to the door. I could see that it was locked—he had to take out his passkey to open it. Then, the instant he swung the door open, the lights went out. He was inside about five minutes, then came out, locked up, and came over to my place. He said he'd found nothing unusual, and the place was locked up tight. He told me to call if anything else happened, but I didn't see or hear anything the rest of the night. Strange, huh?"

I smiled and nodded, convinced now that my theory was right. I had remembered the night before that we were on daylight savings time—which didn't exist at the time of the war. So 1 a.m. that night would have been midnight to General Barksdale's loyal pet.

Now you might think at first that some type of electrical problem caused the lights to go on and off that night, but all of the wiring was inspected a couple of days later, and no problem was found. As for me, I believed then, and always will, that light switch was being operated by a ghostly paw as Barksdale's hound searched for his long-lost master.

Gettysburg National Military Park is located at 96 Taneytown Road, Gettysburg, PA 17325. Call (717) 334-1124 for information.

The Desert Fox

STONEWALL CEMETERY
WINCHESTER, VIRGINIA

That battlefields are a favorite haunt for ghosts makes sense, considering that many authorities believe that ghosts are spirits trapped between two worlds due to a sense of unfulfillment, having had their lives cut short unexpectedly. Is it possible, though, that spirits aren't restricted by geographical boundaries—that old warriors may sometimes roam, fighting battles other than their own? The facts behind the following story seem to indicate something of that nature.

The years of 1935-39 saw great changes occurring all around the globe. America was slowly fighting her way up from the depths of the Great Depression. In England a king gave up his throne for the love of a commoner. In the Far East, Japan was aggressively expanding her borders. And in Europe, the first whiffs of a conflagration that would soon engulf the world were coming from Germany.

World War I—the Great War, the war to end all wars—had been over for some twenty years. Yet even in peacetime warriors remain warriors, studying other wars to improve their skills. In 1937 a contingent of army officers from Germany, who was then our ally, arrived in America for just that purpose. They visited several Civil

War battlefields and spent some time at the U.S. Army War College
at Carlisle, Pennsylvania. One of the officers was an obscure major,
little known even in his own country, whom the entire world would
soon come to know as the Desert Fox—Erwin Rommel.

The officers, Rommel in particular, were fascinated by the
strategies used by Stonewall Jackson during his famed Shenandoah
Valley Campaign in 1862. The Germans would later apply the
lessons learned from Jackson, the principles of speed and
manueverability, when they unleashed their *blitzkrieg*, or lightning
war, in the North African desert.

During their visit to the Valley, the Germans spent some time in
and around Winchester, Virginia. Not only had the town figured
heavily in the Valley Campaign, it had also been the site of the largest
battle fought in the Valley during the war, the battle of Third
Winchester in September 1864.

While it is not known for certain (who would have paid attention
to an unknown German major?), Rommel could very well have
visited Stonewall Cemetery, the confederate section of Winchester's
Mount Hebron Cemetery. As a matter of fact, the final defensive
line of the Confederates during Third Winchester had been drawn
up through what is today cemetery property. If so, then while
wandering among the tombstones, Rommel may certainly have
noticed one of the more prominent tombstones which is enscribed
"The Patton Brothers."

These two members of an old, respected Virginia family had
answered the call when their native state seceded from the Union in
1861. Each had military training, having graduated from the Virginia
Military Institute, and each would rise to the rank of colonel. Each
would also give his life to his new nation.

The elder brother, Waller Tazewell Patton, was mortally wounded
at Gettysburg on July 3, 1863, while leading his regiment against the
Union army during Pickett's charge. He died two weeks later in
Baltimore, where he had been transported as a prisoner, and was
buried there. The younger brother, George Smith Patton, was
wounded during the battle of Third Winchester and carried to a

house on Picadilly Street, the home of his cousin, Judge Philip Williams, where he died a few days later. He was buried in the town cemetery.

George Patton's son and widow, who lived in Lexington, Virginia, at the time of the colonel's death, found themselves faced with a plight similar to many other Southerners when the war ended. They were destitute and homeless, their once-privileged lives now in ruins. The young widow and her son left Virginia to begin a new life with her brother, a successful attorney, in California.

About six years later, George Patton's son returned to Virginia. In honor of his father, the son legally changed his name to that of his father, and followed his father's footsteps to VMI, not because of his own martial spirit but to honor his father's memory and carry on the family tradition. While a cadet there, George made arrangements to have his uncle's remains shipped from Baltimore to Winchester where, clandestinely, in the dead of night, he was laid to rest beside his brother.

The ceremony was not planned for that late hour, but the train carrying the coffin ran behind schedule. The delay may have been fortuitous, however, as the small band of comrades who carried Tazewell Patton to his final resting place wore their confederate uniforms under their coats and proudly carried the confederate flag, both treasonable offenses at the time.

After graduating from VMI, George returned to California where he undertook a successful career as a lawyer. He married and fathered a son who was named for him, but whom the family called Georgie.

Though pampered and spoiled as a child, Georgie grew up with the martial spirit his father lacked, fueled by the tales of the great War of Northern Aggression and the heroic exploits of his ancestors. He attended VMI for a year and eventually graduated from the U.S. Military Academy at West Point. He fought in WWI, the war to end all wars, making enough of a mark that by the time he and his father made a pilgrimage to his grandfather's and great-uncle's grave in the 1920s, the third George Patton had also risen to the rank of colonel.

However, it was during the next war—World War II—that the world came to know General George S. ("Old Blood and Guts") Patton III.

The world watched as Patton and Rommel dueled in the sands of North Africa. The two greatest tank commanders of their time developed a grudging admiration and respect for one another as each tried to destroy his opponent's forces. Patton emerged the victor, but always praised Rommel's ability as a worthy opponent.

In an ironic twist of fate, neither Rommel nor Patton died as they would have chosen, on the field of battle. Rommel died at his own hand after his role in the 1944 plot to assassinate Hitler was discovered. Patton's death was an accident. Throughout his life Patton had been oddly accident-prone. On December 9, 1945, in Germany, the jeep Patton was riding in was involved in what appeared to be a minor fender bender. Everyone else involved in the accident walked away without a scratch; Patton, however, suffered a broken neck. He died in his sleep two weeks later.

Since sometime in the 1950s visitors to Stonewall Cemetery have occasionally reported an odd sighting. It never seems to happen when people drive through Mount Hebron to the confederate section, but only when they park in the visitors' lot and walk there. They report catching a glimpse of a figure of medium height and build, with an erect bearing, standing near a gravesite some distance away. He is described as wearing a long, gray military-style overcoat and a peaked cap. The figure doesn't turn to face the approaching visitor, but he glances in that direction just long enough to give the impression that the insignia on the front of the peaked cap is an eagle. The figure then looks away, as if afraid to be seen. And by the time the visitor arrives at the spot where the figure stood staring pensively at the tombstone—the gravesite of the Patton brothers—the mysterious man in the greatcoat has disappeared, seemingly into thin air.

Does the ghost of Erwin Rommel, "the Desert Fox," wander the grounds of a cemetery thousands of miles from where he was buried? If it is Rommel, why is he there? Is he searching for his old nemesis, looking for one last battle, drawn to the spot where, at one time, all three warrior Pattons were together?

Who knows? But, if you pay a visit to Stonewall Cemetery and see a figure dressed in a greatcoat, don't be alarmed. It's possible it may only be me. And if the figure suddenly disappears, don't let that worry you too much either. After all, he's probably doing exactly what you are—paying last respects to brother warriors.

Visit the Stonewall Cemetery in the Mount Hebron Cemetery, 305 East Boscawen Street, Winchester, Virginia 22601. Call (540) 662-4868 for more information.

Mad Anthony Rides

BRANDYWINE BATTLEFIELD STATE PARK
CHADD'S FORD, PENNSYLVANIA

It nearly always happens the same way. A car is traveling along a particular stretch of U.S. Route 1 near the Brandywine battlefield in Chadd's Ford, Pennsylvania, around dusk or in the early evening. Suddenly a man dressed in what appears to be a Continental army uniform from the Revolutionary War comes galloping up the road astride a white stallion. The car swerves, and the rider continues on. When the driver looks in the rearview mirror, the road is clear behind him. Some drivers stop at the first opportunity and call the state police to report the incident. The area is searched, but no trace of a horse or rider is found. Mad Anthony has struck again.

The morning of September 11, 1777, found the Continental army under the command of General George Washington waiting expectantly along the banks of Brandywine Creek in southeastern Pennsylvania for the battle they felt was sure to come. Some 18,000 British and Hessian troops under the command of General Sir William Howe had landed at Head of Elk (present-day Elkton), Maryland, on August 24 and had advanced northward in an attempt to capture Philadelphia.

Washington had chosen a strong defensive position. The Brandy-wine, sometimes referred to as a river, could be crossed at a number of fords but appeared to be unassailable otherwise. He placed a division of about 1,600 men under the command of Brig. Gen. Anthony Wayne astride the main route to Chester and Philadelphia, overlooking Chadd's Ford. Nicknamed Mad Anthony by his men in honor of his ferocious manner in battle, the 32-year-old Penn-sylvanian had become one of Washington's favorite commanders in just a few months of service with him. Washington expressed his confidence by placing Wayne where he expected the main attack.

Wayne was supported by two other divisions, approximately 3,300 men, and two batteries of artillery which presented a formidable obstacle. Still, there were no less than seven fords within eight miles of Chadd's that could provide access for the British, so Washington had deployed the rest of his 11,000 men to cover these crossings, ranging from as far as six miles to the north to two miles to the south of Wayne's position.

Unfortunately for Washington, Lord Howe had no intention of marching straight up the road into the teeth of the rebels' strength. One of the great mysteries of the battle of Brandywine is why Washington failed to take advantage of the tremendous amount of local knowledge at his disposal. No less than two companies of men as well as General Wayne were from Chester County and could have provided intimate detail of the area had he only asked. Undoubtedly some of these locals could have told Washington that there were more fords to the north.

Starting off at 4 a.m., under cover of a heavy fog, Howe personally led half of his army on a wide, sweeping move to the north, heading for two fords only two miles above the end of the American line at Buffington's Ford. The other half of the British force, under the Hessian general Wilhelm von Knyphausen, advanced toward the crossing at Chadd's at about 9 a.m. Von Knyphausen engaged in a little subterfuge, marching his troops around and around in a large circle under cover of the surrounding woods and hills, thus convincing the Americans that the entire British army was moving toward Chadd's Ford.

By the time Washington realized the awful truth, it was too late— General Howe was attacking the American position from the rear. The Continental commander stripped the reserves from General Wayne's position and rushed them northward, where a stubborn defense was made by the Americans around the Birmingham meetinghouse, one of several Quaker churches in the area. Never-theless, the British broke through.

As the Continentals rushed to the sounds of battle coming from the north, von Knyphausen quickly struck the weakened position at Chadd's Ford. Despite a heavy fire from General Wayne's troops and those of General William ("Scotch Willie") Maxwell's brigade, von Knyphausen was able to break through. The Americans fell back to a nearby field and orchard.

At this point Anthony Wayne exhibited the ferocity that had earned him his nickname. The fighting dissolved into a bloody, no-holds-barred melee. Wayne rode from point to point in a frenzy, looking every bit the madman he was said to become when his fighting blood was up, as he drove his men to stand fast against the British and Hessian bayonets.

Finally, word came that the line to the north had fallen and Howe's troops were quickly moving to cut off Wayne's embattled warriors from the rear. Mad Anthony gave the order to fall back and began the retreat toward Chester. Still, he gave ground grudgingly, and his stubborn rearguard action played no small role in allowing Washington to escape Howe's trap with the bulk of his army. The battle of Brandywine, the largest land battle of the Revolutionary War, was over at a cost of some 3,300 casualties—1,300 American and 2,000 British.

Even though he would suffer the bitter taste of defeat several more times before the war ended, Anthony Wayne could claim to have won more times than he lost by the time he left the army in November of 1783 as a major general and one of the preeminent heroes of the Revolutionary War. He answered his country's call again in 1792, when he was named commander-in-chief of the American army and given the task of making the Ohio territory safe for settlers. Wayne defeated the Native Americans led by the war chief Tecumseh in a climactic battle at Fallen Timbers, near present-day Toledo, Ohio, in 1794, then negotiated a peace treaty the following year that allowed the westward expansion to continue. The famed commander died the following year on December 15, 1796, in Erie, Pennsylvania, after conducting yet another successful campaign to occupy Detroit.

There are many who believe, though, that Mad Anthony is not resting peacefully in his grave in the cemetery of St. Davis's Church in his native Chester County. Those who feel that way claim that the ghostly rider is, in fact, none other than Mad Anthony himself, still racing along the road that he had ridden all those years ago, trying desperately to turn the tide of a battle already lost. Maybe so. Anthony Wayne certainly was never one to quit—a fighter to the end and possibly beyond.

If you should meet Mad Anthony on a trip to Brandywine and feel the need for some spiritual comfort, you may want to choose somewhere other than the Birmingham meetinghouse, lest you find another spiritual force awaiting you. The scene of heavy fighting during the battle and also the site of a battlefield hospital, the meetinghouse has been the source of many reports of unearthly cries and moans of wounded men. Figures dressed in Revolutionary War uniforms flit by the windows as astonished onlookers question what they saw. I thought you might want to know, just in case.

Contact Brandywine Battlefield State Park at P.O. Box 202, Chadds Ford, Pennsylvania 19317-0202, or (610) 459-3342.

The Gray Man of Waverly

WAVERLY FARM
WINCHESTER, VIRGINIA

If you compliment Kenneth and Tricia Stiles on the beauty and charm of Waverly, their historic farm near Winchester, Virginia, they will smile and thank you in the best old Virginia tradition. They are proud of their land and feel a deep kinship to it. If, however, you ask them about the ghost that haunts Waverly, they will likely ask, "What ghost? We've never seen anything like that here."

While the Stiles's may claim innocence, many visitors and previous owners of the farm know otherwise. Starting just a few years after the end of the Civil War and the death of a young confederate colonel from North Carolina in one of the upstairs bedrooms, dozens of people have reported encounters with Waverly's Gray Man.

During the month of August 1864 the Confederates under General Jubal A. Early played a game of cat-and-mouse with the Federals in the lower Valley, with the Confederates doing a great deal of marching and countermarching in an attempt to deceive the new union commander, General Philip Sheridan. Little Phil was mainly intent on concentrating his large force around Harpers Ferry, pretty much leaving Old Jube to march around unmolested as he prepared his Army of the Shenandoah to reclaim the Valley. As a result of Sheridan's seeming lack of interest and inaction, Early grew scornful of his opponent and scattered his small army of 11,000 men over a 15-mile wide area around Winchester. As he was soon to find out, he had seriously misjudged the true combative native of Phil Sheridan.

At daybreak on September 19 the colonel of the 23rd North Carolina Volunteer Regiment, Charles C. Blacknall, was rudely awakened by the sound of heavy gunfire coming from his picket line along the Berryville Pike (present-day Route 7), about three miles east of Winchester. No stranger to the sounds of enemy gunfire, he mounted his horse and headed toward the sounds of battle to see what was happening.

At the age of thirty-three, Blacknall was a battle-hardened veteran of some of the most desperate engagements of the war. He had been wounded and captured twice, the second and more serious wound received as the lieutenant colonel of his regiment at the battle of Gettysburg. He was shot through the face; his jaw was broken, and he lost several teeth. He was captured, imprisoned at Johnson's Island and exchanged in February 1864. Eventually he rejoined his regiment as its colonel.

Blacknall arrived at the scene of the battle to find his pickets being driven back across the Opequon Creek by the 2nd New York Cavalry. The Yankee horsemen, part of Brigadier General James H. Wilson's division, sent the picket line stumbling back into the main camp of the 23rd North Carolina, where the surprised Tarheels were just starting to realize what was happening. The 23rd fell back to a wide, open plain and began a fighting retreat. During this action Blacknall was wounded in the foot while riding along the immediate rear of his battle line.

The colonel was taken into Winchester, to the home of a Mrs. Smith, where he lay in pain throughout the day. He could only watch as his regiment, along with the rest of Jubal Early's little army, was driven from Winchester. Colonel Blacknall was once again a wounded prisoner of war.

The federal surgeon who examined Blacknall's wound recommended amputation. Blacknall considered the surgeon's dire warning as to what would happen should he refuse treatment, then answered the doctor in the negative, informing him that he would live to dance upon that foot again. He was thereupon moved to Waverly, then the home of a Mrs. Washington, whose sisters were serving as nurses in the town.

Despite the efforts of the doctors and care of the Washingtons, Colonel Blacknall's condition worsened. It was reported that he recovered briefly, his spirits lifting when he heard cannon fire booming in the distance on October 17, 1864, during the battle of Cedar Creek, twelve miles south of Winchester. He asked his servant, Hundley, to dress him in his uniform and gazed expectantly out the window, certain that Early was on his way back to Winchester and that he would soon be reunited with his men. But as the afternoon wore on and the sounds of fighting became more distant and then finally petered out all together, the truth hit home. Realizing that Sheridan had once again gotten the best of the Confederates, the colonel disconsolately returned to his bed.

Blacknall's health went downhill quickly from that point. For his family back home in Kittrell, North Carolina, it was an excruciating period. His wife Virginia, their four children, and his brother George received conflicting reports regarding Charles's health. Finally, in mid-December, the dreaded news came; despite having had his leg amputated below the knee on November 6, Colonel Blacknall had died. He would dance no more.

Blacknall was buried in the Episcopal churchyard in Winchester, laid to rest beside his former commander, Colonel Charles Christie. Later both were moved to Stonewall Cemetery in Winchester, where they rest side-by-side near their comrades from the 23rd North Carolina.

Here the mystery of the Gray Man deepens. If Blacknall's body rests in Stonewall Cemetery, does his spirit still reside at Waverly, several miles away? According to the accounts of those who have seen Waverly's Gray Man, the answer is yes. The room where the spectre is seen is apparently the one in which Blacknall died.

Sightings began shortly after the war when a Mrs. Joliffe, who was visiting the Washingtons, was awakened in the night by the opening of her door. She watched in amazement as a man dressed in a gray uniform walked across the room and stood looking out the window, as if he were waiting or watching for someone. He stood like this for several minutes, paying no attention to Mrs. Joliffe's queries as to who he was and what he was doing. Finally, the man bowed his head as if in despair and turned from the window to leave. He paused briefly at the foot of Mrs. Joliffe's bed and gazed at her for a moment with a sorrowful expression, then left. The description Mrs. Joliffe gave of her nocturnal visitor fit that of Colonel Blacknall.

While Mrs. Joliffe was the first to report seeing the Gray Man of Waverly, she was far from the last. Sightings have continued down through the years, right up to the present. Guests and visitors to the home often comment on the sounds of footsteps coming from the room or on looking up at the window from outside and seeing a man dressed in gray looking out.

For what is Colonel Blacknall searching? Is he looking for his wife and children to come care for him? Is he looking for a dance partner, hoping to fulfill, partially at least, the prophecy he made to the federal doctor more than 130 years ago? Or is he looking for the Confederates to return and once again occupy Winchester, freeing him from his captives?

I hope it's not the latter. If so, judging by Jubal Early's lack of success against Sheridan the first time around, the colonel is unfortunately in for a long wait.

Waverly Farm is privately owned. It is not open to the public.

Phantom Retreat

Once word gets around that someone is working on a project like
this book, people seem to come out of the woodwork with stories of
experiences they have had. You're never quite sure where your next
story will come from or who will tell it. I thought I had overcome my
surprise at hearing stories from people I never suspected of having
had a ghostly experience.

Still, you can imagine my reaction when my wife Jill said to me one
morning, "Maybe you would like to put something in there about the
time I saw the retreat from Gettysburg."

Was I surprised? Dumbfounded was more like it. Marriage is not
a mandate to share everything you've ever seen or done with your
mate, but still, here was something new. "Why haven't you told me
about this before?" I asked.

"I wasn't sure you would believe me until you started collecting all
of these stories," she replied, "but I found out afterward that a
number of people have had the same experience."

"Sweetheart, you know I'd believe anything you told me," I assured
her. "Tell me what happened."

"Well," she began, "it was in 1991, when we lived in the house on West Middle Street, down below the seminary."

During the battle a portion of the confederate battle line ran along Middle Street and turned down Seminary Ridge, where the road intersects the ridgeline. From Seminary Ridge westward, Middle Street is known as the Fairfield Pike, present-day Route 116. It was along this road that most of the 17-mile-long wagon train of wounded Confederates traveled as Lee began his retreat on July 4, 1863.

"It was the night of July 5. I'll never forget the date, because when I thought about it the next day it struck me as odd that I would have experienced this on the 5th, not the 4th. I found out later that the retreat continued through the 5th.

"Anyway, it was a hot night, all of the doors and windows were open. My bedroom was downstairs, and Billy and Katie's bedroom was on the second floor. Billy was four years old and Katie was two.

"About 2 a.m., Katie woke me up. She was crying and screaming, just really pitching a fit. I tore upstairs to see what was wrong. Billy was sound asleep—you know Billy, he sleeps through anything—but Katie was sitting up in bed, looking absolutely terrified. She was babbling, 'Whatsit, Mommy, whatsit? Whatsit, Mommy?' I didn't see or hear anything unusual. I finally got her calmed down and back to sleep after about fifteen minutes.

"The house had a door that faced west, looking up toward the seminary. I had to walk past it to get back to my bedroom, and I checked to make sure the screen door was latched. I stood in the doorway for a few minutes, just getting some fresh air before going back to bed.

"As I stood there enjoying the quiet—the fourth of July holiday was over and most of the tourists were gone—I heard a low noise, just loud enough to be aware of it. It got slightly louder, sounded like someone moaning.

"Then I realized it was more than one sound—as it got louder, it sounded like several people moaning. It seemed to be coming from down along Seminary Ridge. It continued to get louder and became more than just moans. I thought I could hear cries also.

"By then, I guess I'd been standing there for three or four minutes. That was when I realized I wasn't just dreaming or hallucinating. It wasn't something that I heard for just a few seconds or could have imagined. It went on and on.

"Then I began to hear a creaking sound. I was starting to think that there must have been an accident on West Confederate Avenue and I was hearing people that had been hurt, so I stepped outside into the yard to see if I could see any lights. It was 2:45 a.m., and I thought that if there had been an accident, it was possible no one else knew about it yet. I hadn't heard a crash or anything, and it sounded like hundreds of people, not just a few, but what else could it be?

"I saw something, all right, but it wasn't something I would dial 911 about. There was a line of wagons coming up Seminary Ridge and turning down Route 116. They were moving slowly, and I could hear the groans and moans distinctly. There were riders on horseback beside the wagons, and I could occasionally make out someone sitting up in the wagons or see an arm being raised. That's when I had to admit to myself I was seeing something that couldn't be—I was watching the Confederates retreat from Gettysburg!"

"You saw this?" I asked. "You didn't just hear it? I told you I've been up on Oak Ridge, where Iverson's Pits are and heard the wind hitting the stone wall there and how it sounds just like a human moaning. It wasn't windy that night? You actually saw something?"

Jill shook her head vigorously. "It wasn't windy. It was as still and as humid as could be, and, yes—I saw it. Not something. I saw the retreat!"

"I guess you were pretty scared," I ventured.

"No-o-o," she said slowly, "no, that's part of what was so weird about it. I wasn't scared. Sure, since then when I think about it, it scares me. I'm getting goosebumps just talking about it now. But at the time it was more disturbing than scary. That's the best way I know to describe it—it was very disturbing.

"I watched the wagons go by for three or four minutes. Then they stopped, as if the last one had turned down the road or there was a break in the wagon train. It wasn't like they were there and then just faded away. It was more like they just stopped coming.

"I could still hear them, although the moans grew fainter, like they were moving away. I went back inside, yet I heard them for another minute or so. Then it stopped—just like that. That was pretty weird, too. The sound didn't fade away or move out of hearing range; it was more like now you hear it, now you don't.

"Needless to say, I didn't sleep much that night. I lay there, trying to not think about it, but I just couldn't get it out of my mind. When I got up in the morning, I was hoping it would just go away, that I would realize I had been dreaming and forget all about it. But I remembered the sound of those moans so vividly.

"After a couple of days I told a friend what had happened, someone who knew the town well, and he assured me that I wasn't the only one to have experienced the retreat. I was so relieved to hear someone tell me I wasn't crazy or just seeing and hearing things. It wasn't that I didn't believe in ghosts, but what I saw and heard—well, it was a bit much."

I contacted one of the people who had had a similar experience, and he confirmed much of what Jill told me. He is well known within the Civil War community, but has asked to remain nameless because of his often-voiced disbelief in ghosts. He admitted privately, however, that it did happen. Like Jill, he said it had been upsetting at the time, then tried to explain it away by saying he'd been drinking. He said he'd sworn off that brand and had seen nothing since.

Interestingly, his closing comment also echoed one of Jill's. "I never saw or heard it again after that night," she'd said. "Even though we lived in that house for another year and I was there the same date a year later." Perhaps the wagons roll only once for their human audience.

So, if you find yourself in Gettysburg late some July night and see and hear a ghostly column of men in agony, don't be afraid. Go ahead and believe what your eyes and ears are telling you and consider yourself fortunate, since you will be witnessing a sight that not everyone can see. You won't be dreaming, and you may not see it again.

> *Gettysburg National Military Park is located at 96 Taneytown Road, Gettysburg, Pennsylvania 17325. Call (717) 334-1124 for park hours and further information.*

Witness to Battle

KERNSTOWN BATTLEFIELD
KERNSTOWN, VIRGINIA

Ghosts seem to appear to people in all walks of life, yet some with heightened perceptive powers are privy to more complex experiences than merely glimpsing a spectre on a stair or feeling a cold spot in a room. Those who have the gift often have no control over it. An image might appear to them anywhere, at any time. In the case of Dawn Haun of Winchester, Virginia, it happened while she was driving along a country road.

Dawn is friendly and outgoing, with a quick smile and gentle laughter, a real people person. There is nothing of the stereotypical psychic about her—no flowing robes or large hoop earrings, no mumbled incantations and tightly closed eyes. Yet there is no denying that she has psychic abilities. Growing up in nearby Berryville, Virginia, in a house that stood on land that once belonged to Soldier's Rest, the estate of Revolutionary War general Daniel Morgan, she feels she may have been visited often by the general's ghost. On one occasion she viewed a spectral knighting ceremony in Notre Dame Cathedral in Paris. But none of her experiences before or after compares with the day she witnessed Stonewall Jackson's defeat at the battle of Kernstown in March 1862.

As winter gave way to early spring in mid-March of 1862 Jackson, with less than 4,000 men, was encamped near Mount Jackson, forty-two miles south of Winchester, along the Valley Pike (present-day Route 11). He had evacuated Winchester when Major General Nathaniel Banks's army of 25,000 Federals moved from their winter quarters at Harpers Ferry and on March 11 claimed the town. Now Jackson planned to reclaim the lower Shenandoah Valley.

On March 21, Jackson received word from his cavalry commander, Colonel Turner Ashby, that Brigadier General James Shields had left Strasburg with his 9,000 men and were headed north toward Winchester. Jackson surmised that this could only mean that Banks was preparing to leave the Valley and head east to join General McClellan in preparation for the coming spring campaign to capture Richmond, an eventuality that Jackson had been ordered to prevent. Jackson set out after Shields with the famed Stonewall Brigade leading the way. By the night of March 22, the Confederates had reached Cedar Creek, some twelve miles south of Winchester. The pace had been brutal, even for the seasoned members of Jackson's foot cavalry, and as many as a thousand confederate troops had fallen out along the march. It was a loss the Confederates would feel all too soon.

The pace was somewhat more sedate the next day, though still plenty brisk enough for men who had marched twenty-six miles the day before. The Confederates advanced another ten miles, stopping at Kernstown, just four miles south of Winchester. The grateful troops began to fall out and prepare to make camp, feeling safe in the knowledge that the religious Jackson would do no more on a Sunday. One can imagine their dismay when word passed through the ranks to form up and prepare to attack. How could Jackson possibly expect them to fight after such a grueling march—and on the Sabbath to boot?

Jackson hadn't forgotten what day it was, but as he later wrote to his wife, he found himself faced with a situation he couldn't ignore.

Turner Ashby had informed him that no more than four of Shields's regiments stood between Jackson and the main body of the enemy at Winchester. Jackson had to strike quickly to deny the Federals the time to reinforce and fortify their positions through the night.

The fighting began around 3:30 p.m, when the Confederates—Colonel Samuel Fulkerson's two regiments followed by the Stonewall Brigade under Brigadier General Richard Garnett—filed off the Valley Pike to the west and headed for a ridge that might enable them to move around the flank of the Federals blocking the pike. As artillery on both sides began exchanging shots, Fulkerson crested the ridge and moved through a clearing toward a stone wall. Union soldiers appeared from the woodline on the other side of the clearing, and a literal footrace for the protection of the wall ensued. It was won by the Confederates, who unleashed a deadly volley on the Federals before they could turn back for the relative safety of the woods.

As Garnett took position to the right of Fulkerson, the battle was joined in earnest. Wave after wave of union soldiers threw themselves against the Confederates. Before long, an aide brought the unpleasant truth to Jackson: it wasn't four regiments he was facing, but rather more than 10,000 troops. Stonewall replied calmly that it didn't matter, as it was too late to change things, then looked on as his old brigade stood and fought like—well, like a stone wall.

General Garnett waited in vain for word from Jackson to withdraw from the hopeless situation. Finally, with no orders from above but with his men out of ammunition, Garnett issued an order to fall back. When Fulkerson saw the Stonewall Brigade withdrawing, he had no choice but to follow suit. The Federals were winning the day.

As the Stonewall Brigade began their withdrawal, Garnett saw that Colonel William Harman's regiment, which had been held in reserve, was moving forward. Garnett ordered Harman to halt at a second stone wall and buy time for the rest of the brigade to fall back. When Jackson saw the regiment he had personally ordered forward halting, he was infuriated. He rode into the mass of fleeing men, imploring them to turn back and make a stand, but to no avail.

Exhausted before the battle began, his men had nothing left to give. Stonewall Jackson had suffered defeat on a battlefield for the first and only time.

Driving south along U.S. 11 one day in late March 1982, Dawn was unaware of the details of Jackson's defeat at Kernstown. As she told me during our interview, "I had a vague memory that something had happened at Kernstown during the war, but I had no idea what. Shoot, at the time, I would have had to stop and think about where Kernstown was. It was early afternoon on a beautiful early spring day—the trees were just starting to show some green, patches of green were starting to appear through the browns in the fields, and the whole earth seemed to be reawakening from winter. It was warm, almost balmy, so I had my window open.

"Just after I passed the Rubbermaid plant [which is almost exactly at the Kernstown town line], I noticed a strong, almost over-powering, sulfuric odor. I looked around, thinking it had to be coming from one of the buildings nearby. That's when I noticed that something really strange had happened.

"The landscape around me had changed. Buildings that I knew should be there weren't, and across what had become open fields I could see some buildings that aren't there today. Just as soon as this started to register with me, I heard loud booming and knew immediately—don't ask me how I knew, I just did—that it was cannon firing.

"In the next instant, I could see them. I watched the flame shoot out of the end of the barrels and heard the tremendous roar. Clouds of smoke billowed out. I realized then what I had been smelling— black powder. At about the same time that I became aware of the cannon, I began to see soldiers, both Rebels and Yankees, lined up and firing at each other. Then I noticed that the road seemed to have disappeared. It was really strange, because I was still driving—I was aware of that, even though I didn't seem to have any real control over the car; it was kind of like it was driving itself, but I was traveling over the fields."

Dawn's recollections seem to coincide with what actually happened during the battle, since most of the heavy fighting took place to the west of the Valley Pike.

"I saw that the Confederates were retreating. The Yankees were coming from my right [the direction of the actual federal advance], and the Confederates were going south. I realized that even though I was right in the middle of it and could see them, the soldiers weren't aware of me being there. They were running by, riding by on horseback, yelling and screaming.

"That was probably the most frightening thing, hearing the men and horses screaming. As loud as the sound of the battle was, I could still hear them screaming. Have you ever heard a horse scream? It scared me to death.

"As I reached the old stone house that sits on the east side of the road about two miles south of where it all started [Springdale, the oldest standing house in Frederick County], I could see that there was some sort of hospital there. The confederate wounded were being carried back, and there were a lot of horses and riders milling around. Then, as I went past the house, just as suddenly as it had started, the whole scene changed and I was driving along on the highway, just like I had been. Everything looked normal again."

A few months after the experience Dawn visited a friend who has some knowledge of the Civil War. Imagine the friend's astonishment when she pointed out a couple of minor errors on a map of the Kernstown battle—and he had to admit that she was correct. She has since learned more about what actually happened at Kernstown in 1862, enough to convince her that it was indeed the battle of Kernstown she witnessed that March day.

Dawn has told very few people about her drive through time and space since it happened. She was, in fact, hesitant about relating the story for publication. But, as she said, "I realized after that happened and after I had checked and confirmed a couple of things that I saw that day, that I wasn't crazy. I don't know why it happens. It's not something I asked for or can control, I just see things sometimes, and if others can't, well, that's not my fault."

Dawn learned something else that day as well. She closed our interview with a sobering statement: "I also realized that day what a terrible thing a Civil War battle was. I'd never had any idea from what little I remembered about it from school. It was a horrible place to be, and I saw things that I hope I never have to see again."

The Kernstown Battlefield, located just south of Winchester, is currently private property.

The Hessians Are Coming

MONMOUTH BATTLEFIELD STATE PARK
FREEHOLD, NEW JERSEY

During the American Revolution as many as 20,000 Hessians—German soldiers—fought on the side of the British. For many Americans the word Hessian conjures up images of fierce mercenaries in gaudy green uniforms and handlebar mustaches who slaughtered American Patriots. They were, in fact, soldiers from the German principality of Hessen-Kassel, one of four that supplied troops to the British. They remained in the employ of their prince, who leased them out as needed. In a sense they were rent-a-soldiers, much like the security company rent-a-cops of today.

Many of these men never returned to their native country after the war. Some settled here, and others were consigned to lonely graves, as often as not unmarked, their final resting place known only to God. According to one account, however, a unit of Hessian *jagers* (sharpshooters) left not only their earthly remains but their spiritual ones as well on a battlefield in central New Jersey.

In late May 1778 the Hessians under the command of Lieutenant General Wilhelm von Knyphausen joined the rest of the British army as it evacuated Philadelphia. In late June 1778 American general

George Washington received word that the new British commander, Sir Henry Clinton, was headed for Sandy Hook, New Jersey, where he planned to ferry his army across the harbor to New York. If the Americans were to stop him they would have to move quickly.

That same day the Continental army set off from its winter quarters at Valley Forge, Pennsylvania. Even though the winter had been a brutal one, Washington had reason to feel optimistic. The men who had survived were tempered into a lean, fairly disciplined force of some 12,000 men, a number that compared favorably with Clinton's 15,000.

By the evening of June 27 the advance force of Americans, more than 5,000 strong, were concentrated around the village of Englishtown. Washington rode ahead of the main body and met with Major General Charles Lee, who had just returned to duty after five months in captivity. Washington had welcomed Lee back, but the other American commanders did not. They saw him as a caustic, egotistical fop who felt that he, not Washington, should be the supreme commander. Washington ordered Lee to attack the rear of Clinton's column at daylight the next morning and hold the British in place until he could arrive with the rest of the army.

Clinton anticipated a raid on his supply train from the Americans. He didn't have the confidence in the Hessians that he did in the British troops, so when they broke camp at 4 a.m. on Sunday, June 28, he placed the Hessians ahead of the supply train and the British regulars, under Lord Charles Cornwallis, at the rear, which was the most likely target.

The Americans did attack, five hours later. Charles Lee, convinced the Americans couldn't win, had wasted precious hours despite frantic entreaties from General ("Mad Anthony") Wayne.

Cornwallis's rear guard fought well in their effort to hold the Americans at bay until reinforcements could arrive. When the British launched a countercharge, Lee panicked and ordered the Americans to retreat.

As Washington rode toward the sounds of the fight, he was astonished to find his men retreating. When he asked why, they replied, "Ask Lee. He ordered it." Washington was almost beside himself with rage. He found Lee and, in what is said to be the only time the normally reserved future president swore in public, condemned him as a "damned poltroon!" The supreme commander then took charge of the battlefield, halting the retreat with his mere presence as he placed his troops to face the British.

The battle raged throughout the day. Men and beasts sweltered in hundred-degree heat. Mary Hayes, a 22-year-old Pennsylvania girl who had followed her artilleryman husband when he joined the army, spent the day carrying cool water to the thirsty troops from a nearby stream and even lent a hand firing the cannon when her husband fell dead at her feet. She earned the undying gratitude of the soldiers and her place in history as Molly Pitcher.

With the onset of night, the battle ended. The Americans had fought well, yet they had let an opportunity to crush the British army slip away. Washington would have to fight yet another day, thanks to the ineptitude of Charles Lee.

Amid the fighting at Monmouth Court House was one particular company of Hessians. They fought fiercely, and a number of them fell casualty that day, some to American balls, others to the sweltering heat to which they were unaccustomed. The mortal remains of those men who died so far from home were left behind by their comrades who hastened to reach the safety of the ships anchored off Sandy Hook.

In September of the following year a group of farmers who were returning home from a hard day of harvesting buckwheat passed near the scene of the battle. As they walked, one of their number regaled his companions with stories of his role in the American victory. As they crossed a field in the gathering darkness, their dogs began to bark furiously and then dashed toward a patch of woods that bordered the field. They stopped short at the treeline and fell silent, then turned as one and came slinking back toward their masters, their tails between their legs. The only sound from the pack was an occasional whimper.

Curious, the farmers headed for the woods to see what had caused such behavior in the dogs. As they reached the treeline they saw a sight that made their hair stand on end, a sight none of them forgot nor stopped talking about until their dying day. There, just inside the trees, were the Hessian soldiers decked out in their bright uniforms, lined up as if ready to charge. These were not flesh and blood men, but the skeletal remains of the soldiers who had perished more than fifteen months before.

If you find yourself visiting the battlefield at Monmouth Court House when the sun begins to fade, and if you think you see a group of reenactors dressed as Hessian *jagers*, look again. If they seem to be extraordinarily thin, you may learn more than you want to know about this famous battle.

Write Monmouth Battlefield State Park, 347 Freehold Road, Manalapan, New Jersey 07726, or call (908) 462-9616 for park hours.

Brothers-in-Arms

BELLE GROVE PLANTATION
MIDDLETOWN, VIRGINIA

One of the tragedies of the Civil War was the way in which families
were torn apart, making the phrase "brother against brother" an
all-too-often literal occurrence. A well-known example is that of
Mary Todd Lincoln, wife of President Abraham Lincoln, whose
brothers fought and died for the Confederacy. Often overlooked,
though, is how another kind of family was torn apart.

Graduates of the U.S. Military Academy at West Point had then,
as they do now, a special bond, a brotherhood forged by shared
experiences. Old friends, classmates and former comrades-in-arms
met one another on the fields of battle. Some reunions were steeped
in drama and chivalry, some in humor, and others in sadness. One
of the more poignant reunions took place at Belle Grove Plantation
near Middletown, Virginia, after the battle of Cedar Creek—a
reunion that was witnessed by a visitor more than a hundred years
after it happened.

The autumn of 1864 will forever be remembered in the history of
the Shenandoah Valley as the time of The Burning. Major General
Philip Sheridan had been sent to the Valley by General Ulysses S.

Grant to fulfill a specific mission: to clear the Shenandoah of Confederates, then lay waste to the Valley, denying the Confederacy the all-important crops that this fertile region provided. In the words of Grant, when Sheridan was through, he wanted "a crow flying through the valley to have to carry his own provender."

Sheridan carried out his mission in a brutal, matter-of-fact manner, much to the horror of the citizens who watched helplessly as millions of acres of farmland were put to the torch. The pall of smoke could be seen for a hundred miles or more. By the time it was over, Sheridan's men had burned more than 2,000 barns, 120 mills, and had taken or destroyed more than 50,000 head of cattle.

The Confederates, led by General Jubal Early, followed the Federals back down the Valley. They had watched helplessly as the devastation occurred, enraged by the brutality but knowing there was nothing they could do for the moment—numbers and position weighed too heavily in favor of Sheridan.

On October 10 the Federals went into camp along the banks of Cedar Creek, just south of the village of Middletown, and on the 15th Sheridan left his command to attend a meeting in Washington.

Major General John B. Gordon, one of Early's division commanders, disguised himself as a farmer and climbed Signal Knob, a prominent outcropping on the northern end of Massanutten Mountain. From there he could see the entire federal position, and what he saw was a path that would lead around the union left flank. In the dead of night on the 18th-19th, Gordon led three divisions in a single file line to a point on the left and rear of the Union army. Early personally led the other two divisions into position for a frontal assault.

At exactly 5 a.m. the Confederates attacked. The troops of Major General George Crook's VIII Corps literally were caught with their pants down, as many of the men rushed out of their tents half-dressed, the Confederates hot on their heels. In short order the XIX and VI Corps were also overrun. By 9:30 a.m. the entire Federal army had been driven back to a position a mile north of Middletown. All that remained now was for the Confederates to make a concentrated push, and there would be no stopping them until they reached the Potomac. It seemed as if the Valley would once again be in Confederate hands, that they would drive out the Federals just as Jackson had done two years before.

Then—the Confederates stopped.

What happened has been the source of controversy and debate ever since. Early blamed his subordinates, claiming they lost control of their troops, who were busy looting the overrun federal camps. Gordon claimed that Early had called a halt to the pursuit, saying they had won the day. No matter whose fault it was, one fact remains: the Confederates didn't deliver the knockout punch.

Sheridan, who had returned from Washington the previous day and was staying at the Lloyd Logan house in Winchester, heard the sounds of the battle and knew something was dreadfully wrong. In a ride that rivaled that of Paul Revere in American historical mythology, Sheridan mounted his horse, Rienzi, and rode swiftly south along the Valley Pike. He quickly regained control of his army and formed them in a 2-mile-long battle line facing the Confederates, reportedly telling his men they were going to reclaim their camps and would "make their coffee from the waters of Cedar Creek that night."

The afternoon passed with both sides eyeing the other nervously. At 4 p.m. Sheridan finally gave the order, and the Federals swept forward. As he dashed along his line, urging the men on, Little Phil left no one in doubt that he intended to make good on his claim.

Awaiting the union advance on the right center of the confederate line was the division of 27-year-old Major General Stephen Dodson Ramseur. A graduate of the West Point Class of 1860 and native North Carolinian, Ramseur had friends, former classmates, on both sides of the field that day. A month before his graduation, a party had been given in his honor organized by George Custer, a brash, cocky, zealous 24-year-old brigadier general who was one of the most willing participants in the brutal destruction in the Valley, and Tom Rosser, who now commanded a confederate cavalry division. Another party-goer was Henry du Pont, now the captain of a battery of federal artillery.

Ramseur had been married eleven months earlier and had received word on the 17th of the birth of his daughter. As the Confederates crept into position in the darkness, he remarked to General Gordon that he was hopeful of victory, so that he might receive a furlough to go home and meet his new child.

Disaster struck the Confederates when Gordon's division was sent tumbling back. Their flank exposed by the Georgian's retreat, Joseph Kershaw's division also retreated. Ramseur managed to hold his men to their task as the Federals swarmed around his left and hammered him from the front. As he rode along the line encouraging his men, Ramseur had two horses shot out from under him. As he was mounting yet a third, a bullet entered his right chest, passing through both lungs. The fallen Tarheel was placed in a wagon and taken from the battlefield.

With Ramseur down, his division crumbled, and the rout was on. Sheridan pursued the Confederates back through the town of Strasburg. Caught up in the logjam that ensued when a bridge collapsed, Ramseur's wagon was overtaken by the pursuing union cavalry, and the wounded general was taken to Sheridan's headquarters at Belle Grove.

A large and beautiful limestone mansion, Belle Grove boasted an illustrious history even before the war. Built in 1787 by Major Isaac Hite, Jr., for his new bride, Eleanor Madison, the mansion had been partially designed by Thomas Jefferson. Eleanor's brother and future president of the United States, James Madison, had brought his wife Dolley to Belle Grove for their honeymoon. Now, seventy-seven years after it was built, the beautiful home sat in the midst of a bloody battlefield.

Ramseur was taken into one of the downstairs rooms, where he was examined by both confederate and union doctors, who reached the same conclusion: the general's wound was mortal. Ramseur's aides, who had refused to leave his side when the wagon was in danger of being captured, heard the news and gathered around him to await the end.

The room filled with other visitors as word spread. Soon Ramseur was surrounded by old classmates: Custer, du Pont and Wesley Merritt, who, like Custer, commanded a division of cavalry in Sheridan's army. Despite the fact that some wore blue and one wore gray, they came to grieve and say their last farewells to their fallen comrade—their brother-in-arms. Just after 10 a.m. on the morning of October 20, 1864, Stephen Dodson Ramseur died, exactly one week shy of his first wedding anniversary and just three days after having learned of his baby daughter's birth.

Today Belle Grove, a beautifully restored mansion, is open to the public and the scene of much activity. A few years ago, in the late fall, a gentleman arrived at Belle Grove to pick up his wife, a student in a craft class. He arrived early, and as he had never seen the inside of the mansion, he went in to look around. He wasn't a Civil War buff and knew nothing of the history of the place other than the fact that a battle had occurred there. As he walked down the hallway, idly glancing into the rooms, he was surprised to see a number of men in Civil War uniforms, both blue and gray, in one of them. He noticed that their attention was focused on a Confederate who lay on a bed.

An overwhelming sense of sadness seemed to emanate from the room, and it was very quiet. No one spoke, but they gazed with grief-stricken faces at an apparently fallen comrade. Thinking he had stumbled into an acting class engaged in a method-acting exercise, the visitor turned and left.

The following week, his curiosity piqued, he sought out the manager of the mansion and asked about the acting class. He hadn't been able to get the scene out of his mind, and he wanted to find the instructor to congratulate him or her on the skills of the actors who had made such an impression on him. He was surprised to learn that there was no such class. He shrugged it off, concluding that it must have been a group of reenactors. He was from the Midwest and had been warned about those odd fellows who dress up in Civil War uniforms.

About a month later he and his wife were in a bookstore. He spotted a book on the war in the Valley and was idly thumbing through it when he suddenly stopped short. His wife rushed to him, afraid that he was suffering a heart attack as he had become deathly pale. He pointed to a picture in the book with a trembling hand and told her, "These are two of the men I saw in the room at Belle Grove that night. This one was lying on the bed, and this one was sitting beside him."

The photos were of Stephen Dodson Ramseur and George Armstrong Custer. The book had opened to an account of Ramseur's death—the death he had witnessed more than a hundred years after it happened.

Belle Grove Plantation is located in Middletown, Virginia, along the Valley Pike (Route 11 South). Call (540) 869-2028 for further information.

Cedar Creek Battlefield Foundation Visitors Center is at 8437 Valley Pike, Middletown, Virginia 22645. Call (540) 869-2064 for further information.

The Phantom of Fort Fisher

FORT FISHER STATE HISTORIC SITE
WILMINGTON, NORTH CAROLINA

In the mid-1880s, a group of Confederate veterans visited the site of Fort Fisher on the Cape Fear River, the bastion that had protected the port city of Wilmington, North Carolina, during the Civil War. After a day of revelry and reminiscing, they gathered around a bonfire in the early evening and recalled the mournful January day some twenty years earlier when the fort had fallen to the northern invaders. One of the men, looking toward the interior of the fort where the Federals had breached the wall, shouted, "Hey, look there, it's Whiting! It's Little Billy, boys!"

They all saw a figure in a confederate general's uniform standing on the third traverse, gazing toward the sea. The veterans overcame their shock and ran toward the figure calling out, "Billy! It's Little Billy, come back to join us!" But the man in the uniform vanished. It was the first documented sighting of the phantom of Fort Fisher.

When war broke out in 1861, one of the first strategic moves undertaken by the federal government was a naval blockade of southern seaports. Aware of how woefully unprepared the agrarian South was in terms of the manufactured goods and materials necessary to wage war, it seemed evident that if the means of importing those goods could be cut off, it would only be a matter of time before the Confederacy would have to capitulate.

The South's answer was to employ a new type of buccaneer: the blockade runner. These daring seamen in sleek, fast ships slipped in and out of the ports, sometimes sliding right under the barrels of the imposing union vessels that were supposed to stop them. The risks were high but so were the profits for the captains who had the right mix of skill, daring and luck needed to bring a shipment into port.

By late 1864 the blockade had achieved near total success, with only one major confederate port still open—Wilmington. Located twenty-eight miles up the Cape Fear River from the Atlantic, Wilmington was the lifeline to the outside world for the beleagured young nation. And the wedge that held that door open was the Gibraltar of the Confederacy, Fort Fisher.

Built on the southern end of Confederate Point, a peninsula that separated the Atlantic from the river, Fort Fisher is a huge earthwork in the shape of an L. The short side is at the north end, with a wooden palisade, shallow ditch and electrically controlled mine field to guard against a land attack. The long side runs along the beach, facing out to sea. Built mainly of sand and seagrass, the walls are a formidable twenty feet high and twenty-five feet thick. For further protection against bombardment, fifteen traverses were built inside the fort to separate the gun platforms, so that a direct hit on a gun emplacement wouldn't damage the neighboring one. With forty-eight guns for land and sea defense, Fort Fisher seemed all but impenetrable. As long as the blockade runners could slip past the curtain of U.S. naval vessels that lay just out of reach of Fisher's long-range guns, the fort would guarantee safe passage for the cargo ships to finish the short run upriver to Wilmington.

Fort Fisher had to be taken. A joint effort of the army and navy at Christmastime was highlighted by an attempt to destroy the fort by detonating a floating barge loaded with 2,500 tons of black powder near the walls. Rear Admiral David Porter, the union fleet commander, didn't have high hopes for the scheme's success, but anchored the fleet twelve miles away, just in case. The explosion was a spectacular sight to behold, but the net result was failure. One of Porter's officers wryly commented, "Well, there's a fizzle."

By January 13, 1865, the union fleet was back with a joint force of 8,000 soldiers under Major General Alfred Terry. Porter subjected the fort to a merciless shelling, firing 50,000 rounds between January 13 and 15. Under cover of the bombardment General Terry landed his men two miles north of the fort, where they dug in in anticipation of a confederate move from the north.

Confederate Major General William Henry Chase Whiting, known as Little Billy, had been a favorite of his troops since his arrival in November 1862. He commanded the North Carolina defenses prior to the Christmastime offensive, when he was replaced by Major General Braxton Bragg. When the January bombardment began, Bragg and Whiting were upriver in Wilmington, and Col. William Lamb was in command at the fort. Lamb and his cadre of fewer than 2,000 men were heartened by the sight of Little Billy's return until the general announced, "Lamb, my boy, I have come to share your fate. You and your garrison are to be sacrificed." At that very moment, Bragg was making arrangements to evacuate Wilmington, having already written off Fort Fisher as a loss. The men at the fort were not ready to share that opinion, however, and they prepared to defend it to the death.

General Terry began the land attack midafternoon of the 15th. About 2,000 sailors and marines (mostly sailors) moved on the northeast salient of the fort, while 4,000 infantrymen headed toward the northwestern corner. The sailors attacked first, making a spirited assault, yet they were driven back. Nevertheless, their attack was effective, as it distracted the defenders.

As the Confederates along the walls in the northeastern corner of the fort cheered at the sight of the sailors and marines racing back along the beach, a shout of alarm went up behind them. They watched in horror as the Federals poured over the walls on the lightly defended side.

Bellowing with rage, Whiting himself led the counterattack in an attempt to drive out the Federals. The invaders had reached the third of the fifteen traverses inside the fort by the time the Confederates closed on them. Little Billy was in the thick of the fighting, shouting for his men to "drive 'em out!" as he slashed with his sword. He tried to wrest the federal flag from the grasp of its bearer, and as he did so a group of Federals surrounded him and called out for him to surrender. Whiting responded with a spirited, "Go to hell, you Yankee bastards!" and the Federals, apparently offended by the general's ungentlemanly conduct, shot him.

A few minutes later Colonel Lamb also fell wounded. The Confederates held out as long as they could. They fought their way back through and, finally, out of the fort, but the numbers were too overwhelming. At 10 p.m. the battle of Fort Fisher ended when Major James Reilly approached the union line under a flag of truce and said simply, "We surrender."

With Fort Fisher lost, it was only a matter of time before Wilmington fell, which it did on February 22, George Washington's birthday. And with the closing of the Confederacy's last major seaport, yet another nail—one of the last ones—had been driven in the coffin of the Confederate States of America.

General Whiting, now captured as well as wounded, was transported to Fort Columbus, a POW camp on Governor's Island in New York Harbor. Despite the efforts of the union surgeons, he succumbed to his wounds on March 10, 1865. His body was brought back to Wilmington and interred in Oakdale Cemetery. Little Billy, a native Mississippian, was laid to rest in North Carolina with the people he had grown to love and who loved and respected him in return. Perhaps that is why his spirit still walks the ramparts of Fort Fisher in an eternal attempt to protect his adopted home from invasion.

The ghost of General Whiting has been sighted many times over the years. According to Morris Bass, a ranger at the Fort Fisher State Historic Site, Little Billy was reportedly seen as recently as the summer of 1996. A man who was visiting the park just a couple of days after Hurricane Fran had strolled down to the beach to survey the damage from the storm. As he turned back toward the fort, he was astonished to see, standing not four feet away from him, a figure dressed in the full uniform of a confederate general, staring out to sea. As he turned to speak, the general vanished. As the shaken man told the staff at the visitor center, "I don't know how in the world he got that close to me without me hearing him, and I sure don't know where he went!"

Little Billy Whiting is evidently not the only ghostly presence in the vicinity of Fort Fisher. The channel that Fisher protected, which led from the Atlantic into the river, was known as New Inlet. Once a blockade runner had entered the inlet, the captain knew he could breathe easy and enjoy the protection of the fort as he cruised upriver. New Inlet was blocked off and the channel closed during the 1870s. Still, this minor obstacle doesn't keep blockade runners from plying their trade. Many people have reported standing along the banks of the inlet on a foggy night and hearing the paddle wheels of the ships as they head upriver and the whispered conversations of the crews.

There may be a good reason for the whispers. A number of times since the 1940s, people driving along Highway 421 near dusk have reported looking out to sea and spotting a U.S. warship anchored off the coast—a U.S. sailing ship, a blockader still on patrol.

When you visit Fort Fisher, no matter on which side your sympathies lie, take heart knowing you have a friend nearby. If you are from a southern clime, General Whiting will make sure your visit isn't spoiled by a Yankee invasion, and the runners will work hard to supply delicacies to make your evening in Wilmington a memorable one. And if you're from the North, take comfort that the U.S. navy is out there, standing watch just for you, ever faithful.

Write Fort Fisher State Historic Site, P.O. Box 169, Kure Beach, North Carolina 28448-0169, or call (910) 458-5538 for information on park hours.

The War Eagle

Visitors to the battlefield at Vicksburg often comment on the rugged beauty of the landscape overlooking the Mississippi River, the peacefulness of the park, and the more than 1,200 monuments there. Many comments are made about one monument in particular—the Wisconsin State Memorial with its 6-foot bronze statue of Old Abe, an American bald eagle, the mascot of the 8th Wisconsin Infantry Regiment.

A few people have been more than impressed by the bronze sculpture—they've been terrified by it. Visitors enjoying a drive through the park at the time of a full moon, especially on a cool, late fall or early winter evening, have been astounded to see the statue of Old Abe spread its mighty wings and take flight, the moonlight glistening off the fearsome talons and beak, the night air filled with piercing shrieks as he swoops and soars. Local folks try to reassure the visitors. "Old Abe gets a might frisky now and again," they say, "but he's always back where he belongs come morning."

In real life Old Abe was a crafty, crusty, and cantankerous eagle. Born in early 1861, he wound up in the hands of a trader named Dan

McCann, who sold him to the captain of Company C of the 8th Wisconsin in April 1861 when he became too much for McCann to handle. The captain, John E. Perkins, gave the bird its name. The men of the company built the young eagle a perch in the shape of a shield painted red, white and blue, and when the 8th marched off to war in October 1861, Old Abe went with them.

Old Abe and the 8th Wisconsin received their first real test under fire at Farmington, Mississippi, on May 9, 1862. Coming under a heavy confederate artillery fire, some of the men of the regiment sought cover, while others, including eagle-bearer James McGinnis, remained standing. Old Abe hopped down from his perch when the shells started flying and lay spread-eagled on the ground. Several times McGinnis put Abe back on his perch, but each time the young eagle hopped down again and resumed his search for cover. When a shell landed nearby, McGinnis realized that Old Abe had the right idea and flattened himself out alongside his feathered charge. After that, when the men of the regiment saw Old Abe choose discretion over valor, they followed suit.

On May 22, 1863, the 8th Wisconsin took part in the ill-fated frontal assault against Vicksburg. Advancing down the appropriately named Graveyard Road, the regiment, along with the rest of the brigade, was met with a withering blast of canister and musketry from the confederate defenders. Old Abe's bearer, Pvt. Edwin Homiston, slipped and fell. The battle-wise bird began dragging his perch, with Homiston still holding on for dear life, toward the protection of a nearby ravine. Other members of the 8th Wisconsin and men from the 5th Minnesota Regiment followed. The federal troops remained in the safety of the ravine until darkness fell, when they were able to slip back to their own lines. Once again Old Abe had saved not only his own neck but those of his comrades.

Make no mistake; Old Abe wasn't a coward. On many occasions he stood atop his perch in the heat of battle, screeching defiantly at the enemy. He just seemed to have a well-honed sense of self-preservation.

After the failed assault on Vicksburg on May 22, General Grant laid siege to the river city. For over a month the embattled confederate defenders and civilians held out, knowing that if Vicksburg fell, the whole of the Mississippi River would be in union hands and the Confederacy effectively cut in two. Finally, though, they could hold out no longer. On July 4, 1863, Lieutenant General John Pemberton, a native Philadelphian who had cast his lot with his adopted and beloved South, formally surrendered his garrison of some 20,000 troops. Vicksburg and the Mississippi River belonged to the Union.

Apparently no one was more proud of the accomplishment than Old Abe. In a photo taken in Vicksburg with members of the 8th a few days after the surrender, the eagle is standing tall on his perch with his beak thrust upward in a decidedly jaunty, defiant manner.

Like any other soldier, Old Abe knew how to blow off steam and have a good time when the opportunity presented itself. Whenever the regiment was encamped, the eagle was released from his tether and allowed to roam freely, the men confident that his clipped wings would keep the bird from straying too far. Still, Old Abe knew how to create mischief. One of his favorite pastimes was to raid the cookfire of an unsuspecting officer who was looking forward to a chicken dinner, only to have the eagle come swooping out of the sky and make off with the chicken. Abe was also known to help himself whenever he came across an unguarded bottle of wine or brandy.

There are times when a measure of decorum is called for in the military, and in these instances as well, Old Abe didn't disappoint. During dress parades the eagle would raise himself to his full height, spread his wings, and let out a special scream when the national flag or a high ranking officer passed by.

On September 26, 1864, Old Abe was honorably discharged from government service along with other members of the 8th Wisconsin who had chosen not to reenlist. The eagle was officially presented to the governor of Wisconsin as a ward of the state. This remained Old Abe's official designation until after the war when he was reclassified, for whatever reason, as a war relic.

The crusty old bird enjoyed life as a celebrity in the years following the war. He lived in a special room in the state capitol and was often displayed at various political functions and rallies on both the state and national levels. Abe even played a prominent role in the 1868 presidential campaign, stumping for his old commander-in-chief, U.S. Grant.

Old Abe showed his cantankerous and combative nature when a golden eagle named Andy Johnson, mascot of the 49th Wisconsin Regiment, also took up residence at the capitol. The younger bird delighted in tormenting Old Abe, but Abe planned his campaign well and bided his time. On a December day in 1873, Abe launched an attack on his young rival, swooping down on him from above and sending golden feathers flying. Andy Johnson didn't survive. Old Abe had proven without doubt that he was the true War Eagle of Wisconsin.

In February 1881 a fire broke out in a storeroom of the basement of the capitol. The flames were extinguished, but smoke filled the room where Old Abe was kept. For a time it seemed as if the aging warrior would pull through, but the effects of smoke inhalation proved too much for him. On March 26, 1881, Old Abe died.

The veterans of Wisconsin wanted to give their old comrade a full military funeral, but unfortunately the politicians, who had a less dignified end in mind, prevailed. The eagle was stuffed and placed on display in a glass case in the capitol rotunda during a ceremony on September 17, 1881. The body of the famous eagle then was moved to several different locations through the years until, finally, in February 1904, while he was once again on display in the capitol, another fire broke out. This time the entire building was destroyed, a fiery pyre for the feathered veteran.

The spirit of Old Abe lives on today, and not just at Vicksburg. The eagle on the insignia of the world-famous 101st Airborne Division, nicknamed the Screaming Eagles, is none other than Old Abe himself.

So, if you find yourself in Vicksburg, Mississippi, some cool fall evening when the moon is full, don't be surprised if you glance up and see a bald eagle soaring through the moonlit skies.

And if you happen to be carrying a bucket of chicken, it might be wise to abandon it. If you don't, who knows what might happen? The old buzzard always was partial to chicken.

Visit Vicksburg National Military Park at 3201 Clay Street, Vicksburg, Mississippi 39180. Call (601) 636-0583 for more information.

Encounter at Fort Stedman

Petersburg National Battlefield
Petersburg, Virginia

The ten-month siege of Petersburg was a defining point in history. The failure of the Confederacy to break the siege signed the young nation's death warrant. The bloody and static trench warfare developed there became a standard military tactic in the next great war, World War I. And Petersburg marked a high point in the ascendance of one man's star, Ulysses S. Grant, and the descent of another's, Robert E. Lee.

With some 70,000 casualties during the siege—42,00 federal, 28,000 confederate—one might expect there to be a plethora of ghost stories about the place. According to ranger Jimmy Blankenship, a 20-year veteran in and around the Petersburg park system, some unusual sightings have been reported at Fort Stedman, site of the last major confederate attempt at a breakout from Petersburg.

By March of 1865 it was apparent to most people on both sides that the long, bloody war was nearing an end. For more than nine months Lee's Army of Northern Virginia, the pride of the Confederacy, had been stalemated in the trenches around Petersburg. The loss of the Shenandoah Valley the previous fall and

the capture of Wilmington, North Carolina, in February—coupled
with Grant's ever-tightening grip on the their supply lines—had led
to a winter of misery and starvation for the embattled Confederates.
The belated appointment of Lee as general-in-chief of all the
Confederacy's armies in February had come too late to be of any
practical use.

Still, Lee wasn't ready to give in. If he could stage a breakout
somewhere along the 37-mile front around Petersburg, he thought
it might be possible to march southward and join General Joseph
Johnston's little army in North Carolina, defeat Sherman, then race
back to Virginia to defeat Grant. A million to one would probably
be generous odds to place on such a plan, but Lee had accomplished
the impossible several times before.

Lee called a meeting with Major General John B. Gordon,
temporary commander of the 2nd Corps, and outlined his plan. He
assigned to Gordon the task of finding a spot along the line that
would offer the greatest chance of success. It was an awesome
responsibility to lay on the shoulders of the 33-year-old Georgian,
but Lee was confident that if anyone could find a hole to slip through,
it was the man who had engineered the successful flank attack at
Cedar Creek the previous October.

Three weeks later, Gordon returned to Lee and reported he had
found the spot. Fort Stedman, near the center of the union line, was
located at a point where the opposing lines were no more than 150
yards apart. Gordon then outlined a hopelessly complicated plan of
attack that called for pinpoint coordination between infantry and
cavalry. Lee was desperate. With seemingly no viable alternative
available to him, he approved Gordon's plan.

The attack was scheduled for 4 a.m. on the morning of March 25.
Lee placed four and a half divisions, almost half the army, under
Gordon's direct control and promised to rush the rest of the army to
Gordon's aid if the breakthrough was successful. Lee, the gambler,
was willing to risk everything on this high-stakes roll of the dice.

At first the assault went remarkably well. Pioneers from Brigadier
General Gaston Lewis's North Carolina brigade quickly cleared a

path through the abatis and other obstructions built up between the lines. No doubt the Confederates were aided in this initial success by the complacency of the union pickets who, by this time, were used to confederate deserters slipping across the lines by the dozens every night.

Fort Stedman had four artillery emplacements surrounding and protecting it: Batteries Nine and Ten to the north and Eleven and Twelve to the south. The Confederates broke through north of Stedman, between Batteries Nine and Ten. Three columns of Confederates poured through the breach.

Moving in the darkness with relative quiet and speed, two of the columns took Battery Ten and the fort itself with little difficulty. The surprise was so complete that in the confusion the fort's commander, Brigadier General Napoleon McLaughlen, found himself commanding a group of men who he thought were union pickets returning to the fort. It was several minutes before McLaughlen realized that it was a detachment of Confederates and they realized they were following orders issued by a Yankee general. The Rebels rectified the situation by taking McLaughlen prisoner.

The third column, which had turned north to take Battery Nine, did not enjoy the same success, however. Massachusetts troops had formed a defensive wall around the position, and the Confederates became hopelessly entangled in the maze of trenches running behind the lines. The attack bogged down some 500 yards short of its objective.

Having taken Fort Stedman, the right column of the attackers then turned their attention toward Fort Haskell, some 600 yards to the south. They managed to take batteries Eleven and Twelve, and the guns in Stedman and the surrounding batteries were soon added to the assault. With daylight breaking, the need for haste was apparent. As union artillery on the hills and ridges surrounding the fort began to return the Confederates' fire, Gordon, who had followed his men into Fort Stedman, sent word to Lee that all was going well. He then attempted to rally his men for the push against Fort Haskell.

Unfortunately, the momentum of the attack had been broken. The gnawing hunger in the pit of each man's stomach burned hotter than the martial spirit that filled his heart. The men who had starved in the trenches all through the winter gorged themselves on the bountiful supplies they found in the union camps.

The rest of the Federal IX Corps surrounding Fort Stedman were finally aware that something serious was happening. The commander of the corps' reserve division, Brigadier General John Hartranft, began to position his men to seal off the breach created by the confederate assault. By 7:30 a.m., less than four hours after the attack had begun, the hills and ridges surrounding Fort Stedman bristled with union troops and artillery. General Lee, observing the Federals massing for an attack, knew the gamble had failed. He sent word to Gordon to break off the attack and return to his own lines.

Gordon had, by this time, already arrived at the same conclusion. With the federal knot surrounding Stedman beginning to close, the problem now was how to escape. Already the union artillery was laying down such heavy fire between the two lines that crossing back over the no-man's-land would be almost as bad as trying to stay and fight it out. The decision was made for him when Hartranft, with more than 4,000 men, began to advance. Most of the Confederates ran the gauntlet back to the relative safety of their lines. By a little after 8 a.m. the assault on Fort Stedman was over, and the course was set for Lee's date with destiny at Appomattox Court House less than three weeks later.

When the two armies moved away from Petersburg a little more than a week after the attack on Fort Stedman, apparently not everyone left. The Confederates had lost between 2,800 and 4,000 men of the 12,000 to 15,000 who had advanced. The Federals had lost no more than 1,500, yet it seems as if some union troops, or at least their spirits, stayed behind.

Ranger Blankenship says that he has never seen or heard anything strange near Fort Stedman, but he related a story told to him by a friend who has since passed on. "My friend was one of those guys who just flat didn't believe in ghosts," he said. "He was the type who would roll his eyes and walk away if someone started telling a ghost story.

"But he told me that out near Fort Stedman very early one summer morning he saw union soldiers on the ridge where Hartranft's division had assembled. They were formed up in a battle line facing the fort. He was surprised to see anyone there, as there were no living history encampments just then, and there certainly weren't supposed to be any armed reenactors in the park at that hour.

"He said he stood there watching them for a couple of minutes, wondering if he should approach them or call for help on the radio. Then, just as suddenly as they had appeared, they were gone. They just vanished while he was watching them."

Ranger Blankenship's friend isn't the only one to have seen the ghostly battle line; others have reported similar experiences. And then there is the regimental band that plays in the mornings.

A former park supervisor who lived in one of the park houses near the fort reported that on several mornings, always around five-thirty, he was awakened by the sounds of a military band that seemed to be up on the ridge where the IX Corps camps had been. They played popular patriotic songs like "Battle Cry of Freedom," "The Star-Spangled Banner," and "John Brown's Body." It happened so often that he called it his spiritual alarm clock. Fort Lee army base is near-by, but he swore that it wasn't their band or the base loudspeakers. He'd checked that out.

Do federal troops still guard Fort Stedman? And if they do, are they heartened by a long-forgotten regimental band playing martial airs? Maybe. But if you approach Ranger Blankenship with a report of union soldiers at Fort Stedman, he probably won't be too surprised.

Contact Petersburg National Battlefield at P.O. Box 549, Petersburg, Virginia 23804-0549 or by calling (804) 732-3531. The battlefield is located along Route 36 East.

Strange Doings at Port Hudson

PORT HUDSON STATE COMMEMORATIVE AREA
ZACHARY, LOUISIANA

By the spring of 1863, the Yankee gunboats had all but closed the Mississippi River to southern traffic, effectively dividing the Confederacy. Only two ports remained open: Vicksburg in Mississippi and Port Hudson in Louisiana. Of the two, Vicksburg was considered to be the more important, yet each depended on the other to keep open the stretch of river between them.

Port Hudson is all but overlooked in many histories of the war, but it was unforgettable to the troops who fought there. That vivid memory may explain why some of the men—or at least their spirits— apparently never left. According to a number of reports, Port Hudson is a hotbed of ghostly activity.

The Federals needed to secure the entire river to prevent the Confederates from moving supplies to the west, so General Ulysses S. Grant took his federal forces to Vicksburg, and General Nathaniel P. Banks turned his attention on Port Hudson.

A former Speaker of the House and the governor of Massachusetts when war broke out, Banks had earned his rank on the basis of the number of men and supplies he provided to the Union rather than his battlefield performance. He had lost so many supplies to Stonewall Jackson in the Shenandoah Valley the year before that the Confederates had nicknamed him Commissary Banks. His reputation would improve, Banks believed, if he could take the prize of Port Hudson without help.

By May 23 Banks had maneuvered his army of roughly 30,000 men into position north of the city. It seemed impossible that the 7,000 Confederates of Major General Franklin Gardner could hold out very long despite their strong defensive position. They couldn't escape to the west, as Admiral David Farragut's gunboats controlled the river above and below the rebel position. A quick, decisive push, Banks decided, would force Gardner to surrender or be swept over the 100-foot bluffs that made the stronghold nearly impregnable.

In his first direct assault on May 27 Banks learned that the confederate earthworks and barricades were every bit as strong as they appeared to be at first glance. By the time he called off the attack, the Federals had suffered some 2,000 casualties compared to 200 for the defenders. He began to realize that this wasn't going to be so easy after all.

About this time General William Emory, commander of the federal garrison at New Orleans, requested troops from Banks to help in the defense of that city. Emory was convinced that confederate general Richard Taylor, who was operating openly in Banks's rear, was going to swoop in and reclaim New Orleans for the Confederacy. Banks, now obsessed with capturing Port Huron, refused the request, telling Emory to look to the navy for help. Don Quixote had found his dragon.

The siege continued, with the heat and malaria of the Louisiana swamps and river bottoms taking its toll, sapping any enthusiasm the men may have had for their work. Morale waned on the confederate side, and deserters began to filter into the union camps. Enlistments were running out among the Federals, and the men on that side clamored to go home.

Banks made another all-out effort to take his objective on June 13. He laid down a heavy, day-long artillery bombardment, concentrating his own firepower and that of the navy in hopes of blasting the stronghold to oblivion, yet his demand for surrender at day's end was refused. Convinced that Gardner couldn't withstand another attack, Banks ordered another frontal assault the next day.

If the attack on May 27 had been ill-advised, this second effort was epic in its failure. Wave after wave of Federals threw themselves against the confederate position and were cut down unmercifully. By the time it was over, Banks had lost 1,800 men to Gardner's 47—the most one-sided defeat of the entire war.

Banks knew that he would probably face open mutiny should he try to order another assault, so the siege continued. By June 29 the rebel deserters that were trickling in reported that the only meat left to the garrison were the mules.

Vicksburg fell on July 4, sealing the fate of Port Hudson. On July 8 General Gardner received confirmation of the loss. With the outcome and fate of his own men now truly inevitable, Gardner surrendered on July 9. After forty-eight days—the longest continuous siege with no outside relief during the entire war—Port Hudson capitulated. The Mississippi River belonged to the federal government once again, and together with Lee's repulse earlier in the week at Gettysburg, the Confederacy had suffered blows from which it would never recover.

Today the state park at Port Hudson comprises some 650 acres of the original battlefield. An interpretive walking trail meanders from the modern visitor center through the heart of the Confederate positions, and an elevated boardwalk spans the site of Fort Desperate, an earthwork that was the focus of much of the heaviest fighting during the May 27 assault. It is a beautiful and quiet spot overlooking the park and the river below, a very peaceful setting.

How peaceful things really are at Port Hudson, though, is debatable. There have been a number of curious incidents that remain without explanation.

Take, for instance, something that happened in the mid-1980s. Late one night a relic hunter and his buddy were working an area that was inside the confederate lines but just outside the park boundaries when something caught his attention. He turned around, and there, no more than five feet away, stood a confederate soldier slowly shaking his head. The frightened man called out to his partner, but by the time the other fellow looked, the soldier had vanished. The two men were waiting to report what had happened when the rangers opened the office the next morning. While the one fellow couldn't admit to having seen the ghost himself, he was convinced his buddy had. "I've never seen him scared like that," he said. "He sure saw something out there."

Then there was the case of a man walking along the railroad tracks close to the northwestern corner of the confederate lines, again outside the park. Little fighting had occurred there, although one man had been killed and another wounded in that sector on May 27. The tracks, built in the 1890s, ran near the site of the confederate earthworks. According to a local source, the fellow in question was a retired businessman, well known and respected in the area; none who knew him would ever question his honesty or sanity. It was his habit to walk along the railroad tracks after a rain and pick up the bullets and other small relics that often surfaced there.

One summer day in the late 1970s, after a particularly heavy rain, he was walking the tracks, his attention focused downward. As he stepped from one tie to the next, he chanced to glance up and found himself almost nose to nose with a confederate soldier. Startled, he stumbled. He reached out, intending to grab the soldier to steady himself, and found himself falling right through the apparition. As he said later, "There was nothing to grab on to but a blast of icy air." When he righted himself, he turned to where the soldier had been, but there was nothing to see but the railroad tracks stretching out into the distance.

Yet another incident involved a park ranger who spent the night at the ranger station at Fort Desperate in the early 1990s. The station is built near the site of the camp of the 15th Arkansas Regiment. He didn't get much sleep that night as he was disturbed several times by the sounds of voices and people moving about outside. Each time he hauled himself up and went out to see who was there, yet no one was to be found—nor were there any tracks visible in the dew-dampened grass. Who was there? He doesn't know.

Then there is the case of the two soldiers, one from each side, who were buried in the same grave. Port Hudson has a national cemetery where the union dead are interred. Most of the Confederates were buried in the town cemetery, which over the years has suffered from erosion and changes in the river's course. At one point nature threatened to wash away the confederate section. A plan to establish a cemetery for the Confederates within the park's boundaries was proposed, and a team of archaelogists arrived to study the feasibility of moving the Confederates.

During the dig a confederate and a union soldier were discovered lying side by side. No one knew how the two came to be buried in such a manner, but a local leading citizen suggested it would be a fitting tribute to rebury the two in a common coffin, with a monument to memorialize this final bonding and healing of old wounds. The money was raised, the monument commissioned and the site, just outside the vistor center at the park, was readied.

The day came for the burial and dedication of the monument—a beautiful summer day with not a cloud in the sky. The solemn ceremony proceeded smoothly until the coffin was lowered into the grave that had been prepared for it. Suddenly, with no warning, groundwater flooded into the hole, and the coffin floated to the top. The grave was bailed out, enough dirt was packed in to stop the seepage, and the ceremony concluded at about 3:30 p.m.

When the site manager walked back into his office, he noticed something strange. On the wall was a picture of his ancestor—a Confederate who had served at Port Hudson during the siege. The picture was trembling, as if an earthquake were rattling it, yet nothing else in the office was moving. As the mystified manager looked on, the picture jumped from the wall as if thrown and landed facedown on the floor.

Less than fifteen minutes later, the ranger reported, the beautiful, cloudless day was abruptly altered by "the biggest, meanest, blackest thunderstorm I've ever seen. The sun was blazing one minute, and in a matter of seconds—not minutes, but seconds—a storm appeared out of nowhere."

While everyone stood at the windows and watched, two lightning bolts hurtled out of the sky at almost the same instant. One crashed to the ground just a few feet from the spot where, less than an hour earlier, the bones of the two sworn enemies had been mixed together and buried in the same box. The other bolt chose as its target a majestic old oak tree, one that had certainly seen the two men when they were still alive, and split the tree in two, sending one smoking half falling toward the brand-new monument.

"I don't know that it qualifies as a ghost story, but it sure was a spooky thing to see," a witness said. "I'd say those two fellas weren't very pleased about being buried together!"

And that's not all that's unusual about Port Hudson. Many visitors have encountered a strange phenomenon along the trails that wind throughout the park. Even on the hottest of days, cold spots mysteriously appear. In fact, they report, it's not uncommon to hit several of them within just a few minutes and a few yards of each other. They also report that if they return just a few minutes later, the cold spot will have disappeared.

"People who believe in such things tell me that the cold spots are ghosts or spirits," ranger Mike Fraering told me. "I don't know that I believe that; I'm sure there's probably a scientific explanation for them. One thing I can't deny, though, is that they're out there. I've felt them myself plenty of times." Ranger Mike says he doesn't really believe in ghosts, but even he admits that some of the happenings at Port Huron defy explanation. And if you're there on a hot summer day, remember the cool spots on the trail. They could be refreshing.

Port Hudson State Commemorative Area can be visited at 756 West Plains-Port Hudson Road in Zachary, Louisiana 70791. Call (504) 654-3775 for further information.

The Spectral Scot of Kings Mountain

KINGS MOUNTAIN NATIONAL MILITARY PARK
KINGS MOUNTAIN, NORTH CAROLINA

For the longest time I didn't think I was going to be able to include the battle of Kings Mountain in this book, even though it was the largest battle of the Revolutionary War that pitted Americans against Americans and is a personal favorite of mine. I grew up in the foothills of western North Carolina, near the homes of Joseph McDowell and the well-known Indian fighter John Sevier, two of the principal players for the Patriot side. I stomped the battlefield as a kid and remember being told that the reason the Patriots won the battle was because they charged uphill, and when the Loyalists tried to shoot down at them, the bullets rolled out of their guns. (Amazing the things you remember from childhood—and no, I didn't believe it, even then.)

Then I spoke to a friend who is a Revolutionary War reenactor who portrays a soldier in the 42nd Highland Regiment of Foot, the famed Black Watch Regiment. He said, "Call this fellow I know. He had an experience there, but he doesn't usually talk about it."

I called, introduced myself, and said why I was calling. The voice on the other end went silent for a moment, then said, "I'll get back to you." After checking with my friend, the gentleman did call back and, with my promise that he would remain anonymous, he told me the story. He then gave me the telephone number of the fellow who had been with him, who confirmed the story, detail by detail, under the same condition of total anonymity. Theirs was one of the most interesting stories I collected for this book.

Today, when an ardent Southerner refers to the Civil War as the "Second War for Independence," he or she is entirely correct. The Revolutionary War, especially in the South, was a bloody, bitter, merciless civil war, pitting friends and family against one another. Without question, loyalties to the respective causes were every bit as strong, and men and women were just as willing to kill or be killed for their beliefs as their descendants would be eighty years later.

The year 1780 was a momentous one in the course of the Revolutionary War, especially for the people living in the South. The commander of the British forces in America, Sir Henry Clinton, had suffered a series of setbacks in the North the previous year and now planned to take the war to the South, hoping to draw on the considerable loyalist support thought to be prevalent there for men and supplies, then march northward through the Carolinas and into Virginia.

After capturing the port of Charleston, South Carolina, in early May, the first major objective in his southern campaign, Clinton returned to New York. He left his capable second-in-command, Lord Cornwallis, to continue the southern operation. They were confident that the two armies would link up in Virginia before winter and the rebellion would be finished.

By September, Cornwallis appeared to be well on his way to accomplishing his mission. South Carolina was effectively under British control, and the British were ready to roll northward into North Carolina. However, an incident that had occurred four months earlier would have a brutal effect on the outcome of Cornwallis's campaign.

On May 29, 1780, in the Waxhaws region, on the state line between the Carolinas, Patriots of the 3rd Virginia Regiment under

Colonel Abraham Buford had been surrounded by Lieutenant Colonel Banastre Tarleton's Legion. Whether what occurred that day was a deliberate act or an unfortunate accident is still debated. When the Patriots showed the white flag of surrender, Tarleton spurred his horse forward, drawing his sword as he did so. Did he mean to refuse the surrender and cut the flag of truce from the bearer's grasp? No one knows, but before he reached the Patriot line, a shot rang out, killing his stallion.

His men, especially the loyalist Tories, went on a rampage, mercilessly killing and wounding the hapless Patriots, ignoring all pleas for quarter (for mercy). When it was over, 113 of the Patriots lay dead and 203 were prisoners—with more than 150 of the latter so badly wounded they couldn't be moved. Many of the wounds had been inflicted by bayonets after the men had thrown down their arms and tried to surrender. The total loss for Tarleton's Legion was 19 men killed and wounded.

To the outraged Patriots of the South, the massacre at Waxhaws meant the war had entered a new and terrible phase, and a new slogan—"Tarleton's Quarter"—was on the lips of every southern Patriot. From then on, whenever Loyalists heard that terrifying cry raised on a battlefield, they knew exactly what it meant: take no prisoners, no quarter asked and none given.

After a series of skirmishes and small battles over the summer, Cornwallis strengthened his control of South Carolina and turned northward. On September 25 he occupied Charlotte, North Carolina, and awaited word from Patrick Ferguson, a relatively young British major from Scotland who had been sent to enlist the support of Loyalists in the western part of the state.

The 35-year-old Ferguson had been in the service of the king for more than half his life, having purchased his commission in the Scots Greys as a junior officer by his fifteenth birthday. During a brief posting in the American colonies, he had been introduced to the devastatingly effective long rifle favored by the backwoodsmen. With talk of rebellion in the air, he had returned to England and invented a weapon to compete with the accuracy and range of the frontier weapon—a breech-loading rifle. Despite an impressive test before the king in the summer of 1775, Ferguson's rifle was considered so revolutionary that few of them were manufactured, and fewer still were used during the war.

Back in America in 1780, the intelligent and personable Ferguson recruited and trained as many as 4,000 Loyalists at his camp a few miles east of the British stronghold at Ninety Six, South Carolina. He had a winning way with the Americans, even though he considered them to be his inferiors. Even Patriots were, at first, taken by his charms. Before long, however, Ferguson came to be viewed as a merciless despot.

Despite the current success, the subjugation of South Carolina had not gone totally unchallenged. Tories trained by Ferguson plundered and looted their neighbors, usually without the major's knowledge, while mountain partisans under colonels Charles McDowell and Isaac Shelby staged their own raids against Ferguson's men. Ferguson had pursued the partisans as far north as Gilbert Town (present-day Rutherfordton) in North Carolina, but the mountaineers had by then slipped back into the recesses of the Blue Ridge to rest and recruit reinforcements.

Before moving to his next camp, Old Fort in the Blue Ridge foothills, Ferguson sent an ultimatum to Colonel Shelby, stating that if the rebels didn't "desist from their opposition to the British arms and take protection under his standard, he would march his army over the mountains, hang their leader, and lay the country waste with fire and sword." Ferguson had thrown down the gauntlet.

The partisans, who had faced everything from raids by Native Americans to starvation and death from the brutal elements, weren't cowed by the challenge. Men all over the mountains answered the call. To them, it was a simple matter: kill or be killed.

A force of more than a thousand men gathered at Sycamore Shoals, led by men such as McDowell, Colonel William Campbell of Virginia, John Sevier, and Benjamin Cleveland. Many were unwilling to leave their families unprotected, so they brought them along. On September 26 the Over Mountain Men set out after Ferguson, vowing to rid the countryside of the tyrant who threatened their homes.

On September 30, at Quaker Meadows (near Morganton, North Carolina), the Patriots were joined by Colonel McDowell's brother, Major Joseph McDowell, and reinforcements that brought their numbers to more than 1,400. The little army elected Colonel Campbell to lead them.

Ferguson, looking to throw the Patriots off his scent, had led his troops southward in the general direction of their home base near Ninety Six, then turned back toward Charlotte and Cornwallis. The ruse worked. The Patriots lost his trail and had to send 700 of their best men and horses racing southward to find him. At Cowpens, South Carolina, the column was met by reinforcements from South Carolina and Georgia and learned from Joseph Kerr, a patriot spy, that Ferguson's men were going into camp at Kings Mountain. With no time to lose, 940 men set out almost immediately, intent on preventing their quarry from slipping away. Ferguson sent word to Cornwallis requesting reinforcements—a plea that was ignored.

Ferguson further enraged his pursuers and the populace loyal to the cause of liberty with a proclamation dated October 1 and addressed to "the Inhabitants of North Carolina."

... I say, if you wish to be pinioned, robbed, and murdered, and see your wives and daughters, in four days, abused by the dregs of mankind—in short, if you wish or deserve to live and bear the name of men, grasp your arms and run to camp. The Backwater men have crossed the mountains; McDowell, Hampton, Shelby, and Cleveland are at their head, so that you know what you have to depend upon. If you choose to be pissed upon forever and ever by a set of mongrels, say so at once and let your women turn their backs upon you, and look out for real men to protect them.

Pat Ferguson,
Major 71st Regiment

If this missive frightened or shamed anyone into joining Ferguson, history doesn't record it. Certainly none of Campbell's men were frightened off. Rather, in their minds, Patrick Ferguson had signed his own death warrant.

The city of Kings Mountain is in North Carolina; Kings Mountain itself is a little over a mile away, just across the state line in South Carolina. The mountain is, in fact, a long ridge, the crest of which is shaped like a canoe paddle about 600 yards long and about 120 yards wide at the paddle end, tapering to 60 yards wide at the handle end. The crest was treeless at the time of the battle, yet the slopes were heavily covered with trees and rocks. Ferguson evidently thought the ruggedness of the terrain would protect him from attack, since he took no measures to fortify his position. He "defied God Almighty and all the rebels out of hell" to overcome him, little realizing that the rocks and trees that he saw as impediments provided natural cover to the wily backwoodsmen.

By noon on Saturday, October 7, the Patriots were a mile from Kings Mountain. They had captured one of Ferguson's couriers, John Ponder, and had learned two important things: Ferguson had about 900 men on the crest of the ridge, and he could be easily identified, as he would be the only officer wielding a sword with his left hand. (He had been severely wounded at Brandywine, where a ball had smashed his right elbow.)

The Patriots encircled the ridge and started up the slopes. Sevier, Campbell and Shelby opened the fight, pushing up the slopes on the southern, or handle end, of the ridge. Ferguson formed his troops in an open-ended square, applying the regular army tactics he had so diligently taught and drilled into them. It soon developed into a battle of styles: the Tories would fire a volley, then charge the slopes with their bayonets. The Patriots would back down the slopes from the charge, then creep back to the top, employing the irregular tactics that had kept them alive as they forged their homes out of the wilderness. To make matters worse for Ferguson, the high ground that he had counted on to aid him now worked against him; time after time, the Loyalists' volleys flew high over the heads of their attackers, as they were unable to adjust the trajectory as they fired downhill at the Patriots.

Before long the Patriots began to push their way up the broad end of the ridge as well. With his rear threatened and the Patriots gaining ground on the narrow end, Ferguson raced back toward the broad end to establish a new line. Within minutes his parade-ground lines had been pushed into a ragged circle around the main camp. White flags were twice raised by Ferguson's troops, and twice Ferguson cut the flags down with his own sword, vowing that "never would he yield to such damned *banditti*." In what can only be termed a suicidal dash for glory and honor, Ferguson mounted his white stallion and raced toward the patriot line, leading a handful of men. Rifles were leveled, shots rang out, and Patrick Ferguson, riddled with bullets, toppled from his horse.

Hopelessly surrounded, the Tories began to wave white shirts and handkerchiefs in earnest, but it was no use. All over the field could be heard the cries "Buford's quarter!" and "Tarleton's quarter!" as the Patriots took revenge for the depredations their friends and neighbors had suffered. To their credit, Campbell, Shelby, Sevier and other patriot commanders tried to stop the slaughter, knocking aside rifles and calling out for the Tories to throw down their weapons if they sought quarter, but it was some time before the killing was ended. When it was finally over, the Tory Loyalists had suffered 157 killed, 163 too badly wounded to be moved, and 698 prisoners. The Patriots had lost 28 killed and 64 wounded. Waxhaws was avenged, and the threat to the homes of the Over Mountain Men was ended.

Ferguson's body was stripped, and one after another, men came forward and did to his corpse what he had claimed they would do to their fellow countrymen. His remains were then wrapped in a cow-hide and buried in a shallow ravine near the crest of the hill. Stones were piled over the grave to keep wild animals from getting to the body. Over the years more stones were added by the Scots in the area. Ferguson was, after all, one of their own, and a proper Scottish cairn was built on the site. Ferguson was further honored on the 150th anniversary of the battle with a monument erected in the name of the citizens of the United States. It reads simply, "A soldier of military distinction and of honor."

It was at the gravesite that the recent spectral encounter took place, an event that neither military science nor any other science can explain. It was early November and quite cold; the park was almost deserted as the two friends roamed the area sharing their knowledge of the battle. Dusk was closing in fast by the time they reached the cairn, and they were the only ones left on the field.

As they stood by the pile of stones, one of the men remarked that the traditional purpose of a cairn was twofold. The Scots erected them to mark the resting place of an honored person and also to keep the spirit of the deceased from roaming. As they stood there, suddenly, "we both felt uneasy," my source said. "We kept talking, but I had the oddest sense that we weren't alone. I turned, expecting to see a ranger or another visitor, thinking I hadn't heard them approach. My friend later said that he felt the same thing.

"Well, there was someone there, all right, but it wasn't a ranger. About eight feet away, watching us, was Major Patrick Ferguson.

"There was no doubt in my mind that it was him. He looked just like his portaits, and his right arm was bent at a funny angle. The real surprise was the duster he was wearing. It was a long, checkered shirt, like the one that he supposedly wore over his uniform during the battle.

"As long as I live I'll remember the look on his face. He wore a little smile, as if he was laughing at us. He said, 'It doesn't always work, my lads,' then he threw back his head, laughed out loud, took a couple steps backward toward the trees, and vanished. I guess he was referring to the cairn not being able to keep his spirit in.

"The few people we've told ask if we didn't imagine it, if we didn't just scare ourselves with the stories we were telling. I don't pretend to have an explanation for it, but I know I saw what I saw. It wasn't my imagination—it was Pat Ferguson."

There have been no other reports of encounters with Major Ferguson, at least none that have been shared publicly. But who knows? You may want to be careful what you say when you're near his grave. You never know who may be listening.

Write to Kings Mountain National Military Park, P.O. Box 40, Kings Mountain, North Carolina 28086-0040, or call (864) 936-7921.

Hauntings at Harper House

BENTONVILLE BATTLEGROUND STATE HISTORIC SITE
NEWTON GROVE, NORTH CAROLINA

The last major battle of the Civil War didn't involve Lee or Grant; it didn't take place in Virginia. The last major battle of the war was fought March 19-21, 1865, near a little village named Bentonville in North Carolina. It was there that confederate general Joseph E. Johnston and his ragtag army made a last ditch effort to defeat union general William Sherman's juggernaut of more than 60,000 men as they rolled relentlessly through the Carolinas.

One of the best-known landmarks of the Bentonville battlefield is the farmhouse of John Harper. The 62-year-old Harper, his wife Amy and their six children looked on as their home was turned into a field hospital filled with the shrieks and cries and moans of the wounded and dying. The experience left an indelible impression on Harper and his family, and evidently it left an indelible impression on the dwelling as well. Hundreds of visitors have come away from the house shaken by what they have seen and heard there, not because it is restored and interpreted as a Civil War hospital, but because they've encountered the ghosts who apparently inhabit the place.

With the South's hopes of victory growing faint, Robert E. Lee called on General Johnston to work a miracle: stop Sherman. On February 22, 1865, Johnston was ordered to consolidate the widely scattered remnants of the Army of Tennessee with the departments of Florida, Georgia, and South Carolina, and drive the advancing Federals southward to prevent Sherman from linking up with General George G. Meade's Army of the Potomac, which had Lee bottled up at Petersburg, Virginia.

With his forces scattered from Mississippi to Virginia, and given the dilapidated state of the Confederacy's transportation system, the fact that Johnston was able to concentrate 21,000 men in North Carolina is testimony to his abilities. Even so, his small army faced the monumental task of trying to stop a force three times its own size.

Old Joe, as the veterans of Atlanta called their beloved commander, saw one possible way to stop Sherman. Due to the labyrinthine road system of eastern and central North Carolina, Sherman had divided his army in two to expedite movement. If Johnston could isolate one of the wings, it might be possible for him to crush it.

On the morning of March 18 Johnston learned that the two sections of Sherman's army were at least a day's march apart. Lieutenant General Wade Hampton worked out a plan for the Confederates to isolate Major General Henry Slocum's left wing near the village of Bentonville, less than a day's march away for Johnston's men. The Confederates would still be outnumbered, as Slocum had a force of about 30,000 with him, but it was as close to even as Joe Johnston was likely to get.

It was a mixed bag of troops that Johnston brought to the battlefield of Bentonville, ranging from the hard-fought veterans of the Army of Tennessee to the old men of the home guard to a brigade of the North Carolina Junior Reserves. What he did have in abundance was generals. The list reads like a Confederate *Who's Who*: William Hardee, A.P. Stewart, Lafayette McLaws, D.H. Hill, Robert Hoke, Wade Hampton, Joseph Wheeler and Braxton Bragg. The quality of the men in the ranks may have been questionable, but there could be no doubt that a more seasoned, veteran group of generals to lead them was not be found.

The terrain around Bentonville wasn't the best for a fight, but Johnston made the best of what he had. On the 18th, Hampton's cavalry spent the day harassing the federal column, buying time for Johnston to concentrate at Bentonville. Slocum's wing ran up against strong resistance as they approached Bentonville on the morning of the 19th, prompting one of the Yankees to comment, "Those Rebels don't drive worth a damn!" Slocum assumed they were facing confederate cavalry once again, but in fact it was Hoke's hard-hitting veterans of the Army of Northern Virginia.

The line formed by the Confederates resembled a sickle in shape. On the right, or handle end, Hoke's division formed a line across the Goldsboro Road and into the trees and swamps that bordered the road to the south. North of the road lay the farm of Willis Cole, with open fields bordered on the north and west sides by woods. The curved blade part of the line ran back through these woods, guarding the approaches across farmer Cole's fields.

The Yankees had their own Jeff Davis on the field, but he was not related to the president of the Confederacy. Major General Jefferson C. Davis, commander of the XIVth Corps, ordered Brigadier General William Carlin to clear the road. As Carlin's three brigades fanned out into battle lines and moved forward, the truth of what was facing them became clear. A union officer raced back to Slocum and Davis with the news. "Well, General," he reported, "I have found something more than cavalry—I find infantry all along our whole front, and enough of them to give us all the amusement we shall want for the rest of the day." By mid-afternoon Slocum had begun to deploy the troops from his other corps, the XXth, under the command of Major General Alpheus Williams, extending his line farther south from the Goldsboro Road.

On the confederate side, General Bragg was nominally in command of Hoke's troops on the left since he outranked Hoke. When the Federals on the right began advancing on Hoke's line, Bragg sent a message to Johnston that he desperately needed reinforcements. Johnston sent McLaws' Division, the first of Hardee's troops to arrive. By the time McLaws got to Hoke's position, the latter already had things well in hand, yet instead of releasing McLaws to return to Hardee, Bragg sent him into the woods and swamps to the left of Hoke, where they stumbled about aimlessly for hours. He eventually sent them back, but it was too late for them to be of any use.

On the confederate right, Stewart, Hill and Hardee led their men forward, smashing into the union line. Slocum, Davis and Williams watched the battle unfold from the high ground by John Harper's house, where by then a field hospital for the XIVth Corps had been established.

Both sides fought well that day, yet each bold advance by the Confederates was countered as the Federals skillfully shifted troops and held them back. Late in the day's fighting Hoke noticed an opportunity to exploit a weakness in the union line. He begged Bragg to let him lead his men into the gap, pointing out that, if successful, the day would be won for the Confederates. Too risky, Bragg intoned, then ordered Hoke to make a senseless frontal assault instead.

Johnston's men had tried, but it wasn't enough. By the next afternoon Major General Oliver O. Howard had arrived with Sherman's other wing, the XVth and XVIIth Corps, and the Confederates knew the battle could not be won.

The Confederates stayed on the field until the night of the 21st, as Johnston wanted time to get his wounded safely away. Sherman was more than happy to allow the battle to end; his objective was to join forces with generals Terry and Schofield, then move on to the state capital at Raleigh. If he could accomplish his goal without the total annihilation of Johnston's army, he was willing to do so. As it was, more than 4,100 men on both sides had become casualties in this, the largest battle ever fought in North Carolina.

When the armies moved on, the citizens of Bentonville were left with the devastation. The Harpers were burdened with the care of as many as fifty badly wounded Confederates who had been left behind. A number of these soldiers died despite the kind and loving care they received and were buried on the Harper farm. For some of them, the war may still continue.

One of the most famous ghostly sightings in the area has been passed on orally and recorded in local writings. It belongs to two hunters who witnessed the battle one moonlit night ninety years ago, some forty-five years after it happened. What the hunters claim to have seen was remarkably accurate in matching the details of the event.

Near the Harper house itself have been heard the groans and cries of the wounded, and soldiers and members of the Harper family have been sighted. A few years ago a worker was alone in the house, yet he felt that someone was there with him. Curious, he searched from bottom to top and found no one, yet the whole time he felt that someone was just one step ahead, almost mocking him. As he headed back downstairs he sensed movement behind him and whirled about. A shadowy figure stood looking down at him from the top of the stairs. He took off running and didn't stop until he reached the visitor center, where he announced that he had spent his last minutes in the house alone.

In 1990 a family from Virginia who visited the park bypassed the visitor center and went directly to the house, where a lady in the group commented on a living history portayal in the rear of the house. It seemed very authentic, she said, especially with the wagons that were pulling up with wounded soldiers. As she toured the house, she also commented that having a living historian portray John Harper made the house visit very realistic. When questioned about this, she said that in one of the upstairs rooms she had seen a man dressed in period costume standing at a window, looking down into the yard. She assumed he was watching the living history performance that she had seen.

Others in the group assured her that there was no living history performance in progress, and no one in period dress was in the house. When asked to describe the man she had seen, she gave an exact description of Harper, and she later confirmed the identification when shown a picture of him. This story, too, has become a part of the local legend.

If you find yourself travelling along I-95 through North Carolina, take the time to turn off and visit Bentonville. It's a battle worth remembering, and you won't be alone, as some of the Harper family apparently remembers and relives the battle to this very day.

Contact Bentonville Battleground State Historic Site by writing to P.O. Box 27, Newton Grove, North Carolina 28366-0027, or by calling (910) 594-0789 for more information.

Rebel Yell

PICKETT'S MILL HISTORIC SITE
DALLAS, GEORGIA

The battle for Atlanta was, in fact, a series of hard-fought encounters that included battles at Kennesaw Mountain, New Hope Church and Peachtree Creek. Often overlooked is the battle of May 27, 1864, which was remembered by many of the participants as the most brutal fighting of the entire campaign—Pickett's Mill.

As the best-preserved and most pristine battlefield of any of the sites involved in the campaign, Pickett's Mill has long been a mandatory destination for serious history students. Though small in size, the reenactment/living history program held there annually near the anniversary of the battle is a favorite of the participants, an event they mark on their calendars and look forward to from year to year.

For two reenactors, a recent event was one they will never forget.

The first two weeks of General Sherman's Atlanta campaign progressed much faster than the union commander had any right to expect, and he found himself more than halfway to his goal. His intimate knowledge of the northern Georgia countryside, a result of having been stationed there in the prewar years, was certainly a factor in his success. In discussing and writing about the Atlanta campaign after the war, he boasted that he knew the country there better than the Rebels did. On at least three occasions, his confederate counterpart, General Joseph E. Johnston, had laid what he thought to be foolproof traps for Sherman, only to see the wily Yankee slip away.

On May 23, with twenty days' worth of supplies in his wagon train, Sherman crossed the Etowah River and moved toward Dallas, a small crossroads town that he thought would put him beyond Johnston's flank. He planned to turn eastward from there and race for the railroad at Marietta. After that, next stop—Atlanta.

Once the Federals crossed the Etowah, though, Sherman found himself in territory that wasn't quite so familiar. With no accurate maps to guide them, it took two days for his army to reach Dallas, and when the lead elements began to arrive early in the morning of May 25, they found that they weren't alone.

Johnston had gotten wind of Sherman's flanking movement and had moved swiftly to intercept him. The Confederates were positioned along a 5-mile-long series of low, wooded ridges that run from a mile south of Dallas to New Hope Church, some four miles to the northeast.

Early in the day Major General Joseph Hooker was ordered to break through the Confederate block and clear the way to Marietta, yet the attack did not take place until 4 p.m. Hooker delayed his move until all three divisions of his XXth Corps were in place. Sherman was furious. "Why doesn't he attack?" he wanted to know. "There haven't been twenty Rebels in front of him all day!"

As it turned out, there were quite a few more than twenty Rebels in front of him. In a fierce fight that raged through a torrential thunderstorm and lasted well into the evening the Confederates held, and Sherman realized that Johnston had won the race to Dallas.

On the morning of May 27, Sherman tried to slip around the Confederates' flank yet again. He assigned the task of finding and turning the confederate right to Major General Oliver O. Howard, the commander of the union IVth Corps.

With 14,000 men, Howard spent the morning and early afternoon of the 27th pushing heavily through dense undergrowth, trying to find what he thought was the confederate right at Pickett's Mill, some two miles northeast of New Hope Church. At one point his skirmish line broke out of the woods into a clearing only to find themselves directly behind a line of battle, looking at the backs of blue uniforms. They had come out behind their own left flank.

About 2:30 p.m. Howard thought he had found what he was searching. He then took two hours to decide what to do, and only then did he deploy his troops. At 4:35 p.m. he sent a message to his immediate commander that pretty much summed up his performance that day: "I am now turning the enemy's right flank, I think."

The federal plan of attack at Pickett's Mill changed at the last minute. Brigadier General William B. Hazen fumed at the confusion but said nothing. He was already upset because Howard had marched his 1,500-man brigade through the dense undergrowth, tiring them out and announcing their presence to the enemy, and had not provided him with artillery to support an attack. He stood by while Howard told Brigadier General Thomas Wood, Hazen's divisional commander, about the change. Wood remarked cavalierly, "Well, we will put in Hazen and see what success he has." Hazen's reaction was reported by Ambrose Bierce, then a lieutenant on his staff: "[M]y commander ... uttered never a word, rode to the head of his feeble brigade and patiently awaited the command to go. Only by a look which I knew how to read did he betray his sense of the criminal blunder."

Awaiting the federal advance were arguably the finest troops in Johnston's Army of the Tennessee, the 4,700 men of Major General Patrick Cleburne's division. To reach Cleburne's lines, the Federals had to cross a deep ravine and climb a steep, rocky slope, the whole of the distance covered with trees and tangled undergrowth. Yet, at 5 p.m. the orders came down from Howard, and Hazen's brigade started forward.

Waiting in the center of the confederate line was a Texas brigade under Brigadier General Hiram Granbury. The Yankees fought well, but they never really had a chance. While struggling through the ravine they were under a constant flanking fire from the rebel artillery. As they fought their way through the jungle-like growth and headed up the rocky slope, the Texans delivered murderous volleys into them from the crest of the hill. Incredibly, some of the Federals made it to the crest, only to be driven down again in a brutal hand-to-hand struggle with Granbury's troops.

To make matters worse, Howard sent his troops in piecemeal. Hazen had expected the other two brigades of Wood's division to be following closely behind him, but they were instead sent in at 40-minute intervals. Each one met its fate unsupported.

As darkness settled over the field the firing ended, yet there was one more attack yet to come. The Texans noticed that a large number of the Federals hadn't fallen back to their own lines but remained below in the ravine, pinned down by the combined artillery and musketry fire. Around 10 p.m. the Texans fixed bayonets and charged into the blackness, giving a rousing Rebel Yell as they rushed down the slope. More than 230 prisoners were taken in the ravine, and the battle of Pickett's Mill was over. Instead of finding the confederate right flank, Oliver Howard had found a way to lose more than 1,600 of Uncle Billy Sherman's troops, at a cost to the Confederates of fewer than 500 casualties.

When one stands today where Granbury's Texans were positioned and looks down into the ravine, it is possible to imagine the fear the union soldiers trapped there must have felt when they heard that famous battle cry and felt the thundering vibrations of hundreds of footsteps rushing at them in the darkness. It is not surprising to hear claims of Yankee spirits inhabiting the ravine after what happened there. In fact, it seems as if some of the Texans have also hung around.

During a recent living history encampment, two reenactors arrived at the park around 11:30 p.m. It was raining, so they decided to sleep in their truck rather than battle the darkness and mud to set up their tent at the campsite a half-mile away. They pulled into the parking lot at the visitor center, which is very near the ravine, rolled out their blankets and pallets and were soon asleep.

About 2 a.m. one of them heard something and shook the other awake. "What was it?" his partner asked groggily.

"I don't know, but it came from the ravine."

"Well, what did it sound like?"

"It sounded kind of like somebody whispering."

"It must have been the wind."

"But there's not even a breeze."

Just then they both heard sounds of movement coming from the ravine, as if several large animals were stirring around in the undergrowth. No sooner had they agreed that it must have been some deer, when another sound was heard. It was faint yet distinct whisperings, as if several people were trying to communicate quietly without being overheard.

Both men were now wide awake and puzzled. As they tried to decide if they should go investigate the odd sound, a loud, high-pitched cry they were both familiar with—the Rebel Yell— came from the direction of the ravine, as well as the unmistakable sound of a body of men rumbling down the hill into the ravine's bottom.

"Aw, heck!" muttered one of the men. "It's just a bunch of the boys out playing. Let's get back to sleep. I'm too tired for that foolishness tonight." His buddy agreed, and within minutes both men were again sound asleep.

When they awoke early the next morning they checked the ravine and were astonished at what they did not find there. The red Georgia clay was still muddy from the previous day's rain, yet there were no footprints, no evidence at all of the activity they had heard. When they took their story to the campsite, their friends swore that no one had left the area all night. There had been no impromptu reenactment of the Texans' charge; no one had even been near the ravine.

If you're visiting Pickett's Mill and it's getting dark, you may want to stay clear of the ravine. But if you should happen to hear the Rebel Yell, go ahead and join in. I'm sure the Texans won't mind.

Pickett's Mill Historic Site is located at 2640 Mount Tabor Road, Dallas, Georgia 30132. Call (770) 4443-7850 for information concerning park hours.

The Dead Angle

KENNESAW MOUNTAIN NATIONAL BATTLEFIELD PARK
KENNESAW, GEORGIA

Atlanta has often been called a phoenix, a comparison to the mythical bird destroyed by flames who rose from ashes to begin life anew. It's an apt enough description. Burned to the ground during the Civil War, Atlanta has risen to become the premiere city in the southeastern United States.

Marietta, Kennesaw and Acworth, once scenes of the Confederates' struggle to prevent the capture of Atlanta 30-odd miles to the south, have become suburbs of the metropolitan sprawl. Many of the breastworks and much of the other land hallowed by the blood of brave men has been paved over to make way for housing developments and shopping malls, yet the national military park at Kennesaw provides an exceptional experience for those who seek to know the history of the struggle for Atlanta.

On weekends and holidays the park also serves as a recreational area. Picnickers, joggers, and those simply looking for a patch of greenery flock to Kennesaw Mountain to enjoy the outdoors. One group of recent visitors, however, found more there than they had expected.

In May 1864 Major General William T. Sherman, in command of three union armies totalling nearly 100,000 men, moved southward from Tennessee into Georgia. Sherman's goal was the capture of Atlanta, the major rail and supply center for the Confederacy in the southeast.

The difficult task of trying to stop Sherman rested on the shoulders of General Joseph E. Johnston. Much of the first two months of the campaign resembled a grand chess match as the two commanding generals jockeyed for position. Sherman was far from being a great fighting general, but he was nothing short of brilliant as a strategist as he continually slipped around the confederate flank, edging ever closer to his goal.

Late May had seen heavy fighting as the two armies slugged it out at Pickett's Mill and New Hope Church. The first two weeks of June found the adversaries reestablishing lines as Sherman tried to slip around the confederate flank yet again and Johnston moved to counter him. The confederate battle line was about five miles long, running from near the hamlet of Big Shanty on the north (present-day Kennesaw), to Kolb's farm, a plantation some three miles from Marietta, on the south. In the middle of the confederate line was the most formidable natural obstacle north of Atlanta, Kennesaw Mountain.

The mountain is actually a ridge with three prominent peaks: Big Kennesaw, which rises 700 feet; Little Kennesaw, 400 feet; and Pigeon Hill, 200 feet. Seen from a distance, the three peaks give the impression of stair steps. To Sherman's troops they must have looked more like the Alps, especially with the confederate artillery frowning down on them from the heights.

The progress of the Union army was slowed by rains that turned the roads into impassible quagmires. After an artillery barrage proved ineffectual in dislodging Johnston from the mountain, Sherman decided to try to break through the confederate line with a direct assault.

Major General James McPherson suggested to Sherman that it might be better to wait until the roads dried out, given the strength of the confederate position, but Sherman was determined. While it seems inconceivable today, his decision apparently was based at least in part on appearances, as he commented to one of his officers that "it was neccessary to show that his men could fight as well as Grant's."

At 8 a.m. on June 27, 1864, the battle of Kennesaw Mountain began. Sherman envisioned a general advance all along his front, expecting to break through somewhere near the right center of the confederate line. He was counting on Johnston moving troops from the center to his flanks to protect against the turning movements Sherman had been using with such success.

Kennesaw Mountain soon proved to be every bit as impossible to take as it had first appeared. While the Yankees were beating their heads against the proverbial stump and making no headway at the center, the fighting was proving to be even more costly two miles to the south.

Near the extreme left of the confederate line two union brigades under Brigadier General Jefferson C. Davis had been given the task of taking a high knoll that was defended by Major General Benjamin Cheatham. Known today as Cheatham Hill, the most prominent feature of the position was the point where the confederate line bent back sharply, forming a salient or angle. When the fighting ended that day, this spot would be known to history as the Dead Angle.

It seemed an impossible task: the Federals had to advance uphill over 600 yards of rocky, wooded terrain, then cross an open field in front of the rebel breastworks. That prospect, plus the 100-degree heat that morning, made many a Yank weak in the knees.

It fell upon the brigade of Colonel Dan McCook, Jr., to attack the point of the angle. McCook was famous throughout the North as one of the Fighting McCooks, a family that sent seventeen brothers and cousins into the ranks of Uncle Sam's armies. Before the advance began, he walked along his lines reciting aloud Macauley's "Horatius at the Bridge." The words "... and how can man die better than facing fearful odds" must have sounded all too prophetic to many in the ranks.

Finally, the order was given and McCook started his brigade forward. As they broke into the open field, the confederate lines came alive with a fire so heavy that one federal soldier wrote, "It did not appear that a bird could have gone through there without being torn into small bits."

From the front, the confederate brigades of generals Alfred Vaughan and George Maney poured out a devastating musketry fire, while artillery rained an enfilading fire into the union ranks. Incredibly, McCook personally forged his way to the confederate lines and leapt atop the breastworks shouting out, "Surrender, you traitors!" Unfortunately for McCook, the men inside the breastworks had something different in mind; a musket was shoved against his chest, and they shot him.

Shortly after McCook fell, the order to retreat passed through the ranks. Few heeded the order, however, realizing that falling back through the open field would be as deadly as the advance had been. Most men simply dropped to the ground behind a slight rise some forty yards from the breastworks and used bayonets and tin cups to scoop out what little protection they could. There they remained until nightfall, when they slipped back to their own lines.

By noon it was apparent to Sherman that his grand assault had failed everywhere along the line. Casualties were more than 3,000, compared to about 700 for the Confederates.

Before evening, however, Major General John Schofield reported that while moving to a position on the union right to make a diversionary attack against the confederate left, he had been astonished to find that there were no Rebels in his front; he had found the way around the confederate flank. By the evening of July 2 the roads had dried, and the chess match began again. Johnston had taken several federal pawns at Kennesaw Mountain, but the confederate king—Atlanta—was still in dire jeopardy.

Today visitors to the Kennesaw Mountain battlefield will find the confederate earthworks at the Dead Angle some of the best preserved on any battlefield in the country. One can stand by them and look down across the open field to the distant treeline and almost hear the desperate cries and yells of McCook's brigade turn into screams of agony as they advanced across that bloody ground into a hailstorm of confederate iron and lead.

During a recent outing to the park a group of seven young men and women—all in their twenties, all professionals who worked in the city and lived in Marietta—heard and saw more than they wanted. They had spent the afternoon tossing Frisbees and footballs, sunbathing, walking along the trails that wind through the woods where the federal assault began, and having an evening picnic. Good friends, good wine—it had been a day of good companionship.

As dusk began to settle in, the group gathered up their blankets and other belongings from the slight hollow at the bottom of the open field below the breastworks. As they walked up the slope toward the breastworks, one of the group commented on the haze that seemed to be drifting over the "Civil War holes up there." Haze and humidity aren't particularly remarkable things in the Atlanta area during the summer, but there seemed to be an unusual quality about this mist.

One of the women pointed out that an uncommonly large number of fireflies seemed to have gathered there. Someone else said that it didn't look like fireflies but more like little points of light, almost like tiny spurts of flame, as if hundreds of cigarette lighters had been flicked on.

Then they sensed movement behind them. They turned and looked back toward the woods, where they saw—what? No one could quite make it out, but they all agreed that it seemed as if a large body of people were moving through the trees. The figures were shadowy, indistinct, so no one could be sure of what they were seeing, but they began to feel pretty uneasy.

Then, within a few seconds of having sensed the movement in the trees, the temperature suddenly dropped. One of the group described it as a sensation of a brisk wind blowing, yet the air around them remained still.

Definitely uneasy now, the group continued on, the happy chatter long since ended. One of the men laughed nervously. "Guess the ghosts are restless tonight," he cracked. Just then they heard a low moaning sound, then a thud and a sharp cry of pain from the field behind them.

Before the sound of the cry had stopped ringing in their ears, the entire group was sprinting out of the field at top speed. As they piled into their cars, they shouted to one another to meet at a local bar.

Over drinks the group calmed down and began to compare notes. After a couple of rounds, they decided that whatever had happened, ghosts weren't involved. After all, they were all educated, successful people who didn't believe in such foolishness—weren't they?

Over the next few weeks the story of the Ghostbusters, as they came to be known to their friends, made the rounds of the local hot-spots the group usually frequented. The closeknit bunch delighted in entertaining their friends with the tale of their adventure, making a huge joke of the whole experience.

Although the group passed off their experience lightly, a few of their friends noticed something interesting: every one of the seven seemed to have other plans whenever someone suggested a picnic or get-together at what had previously been one of their favorite outdoor spots. To this day, so far as anyone knows, none of the group has ever returned to the Dead Angle.

Kennesaw Mountain National Battlefield Park can be contacted at 900 Kennesaw Mountain Drive, Kennesaw, Georgia 30144. Call (404) 427-4686 for information concerning park hours.

The Spirits of '81

NINETY SIX NATIONAL HISTORIC SITE
NINETY SIX, SOUTH CAROLINA

Most states have their share of towns with odd or unusual names. One of my personal favorites has always been one in South Carolina that is actually a model of practicality—Ninety Six. As settlers moved inland from the coastal regions of the Carolinas and Georgia they began to conduct a fair amount of trade with the Native Americans. This commerce led to the establishment of trading posts, one of which was located exactly ninety-six miles from the Cherokee settlement of Keowee.

The rich, fertile farmland around Ninety Six had attracted the largest colonial population of any district in South Carolina. In 1780, when the British occupied South Carolina in the beginning stages of the southern campaign of the Revolutionary War, it was vital to bring Ninety Six under British control. Because of this, a major British outpost was established there.

The British Loyalists who once manned the outpost have long since gone, but local legend tells us that a few Tory spirits may have stayed behind to maintain the king's presence there.

In 1781 the tide began to turn in favor of the Americans when the British withdrew from North Carolina and moved back toward the port of Charleston, yet Ninety Six remained a British stronghold. Major General Nathaniel Greene, commander of American forces in the South, knew that as long as the British remained, the interior of South Carolina would never be truly free. On May 22, 1781, Greene arrived at Ninety Six with 1,000 men, determined to capture the outpost.

The British garrison was commanded by Lieutenant Colonel John Harris Cruger. Like his troops, Cruger was an American, a member of a prominent loyalist family of New York. Of the 550 men under Cruger's command, only one—a Lieutenant Barrette of the 23rd Regiment—was a regular British soldier. About a hundred loyalist families who had come seeking protection and a number of slaves were also inside the stockade when the Patriots arrived.

Despite the great disparity in numbers, the Tory force at Ninety Six was well protected. A stockade encircled the village, and a formidable, star-shaped fort protected the eastern approach to the garrison.

General Greene's record in the Southern Department was a classic example of the old saying, "We lost the battle but we won the war." Since taking command in December 1780 he had lost every engagement, yet undeniably he was winning the southern campaign. However, defeat didn't seem possible at Ninety Six, as Cruger's nearest support was more than a hundred miles away in Charleston.

Greene determined the best way to force capitulation of the enemy would be by siege and began making his preparations. Unfortunately, neither Greene nor his men were familiar with the intricacies of siege warfare.

Colonel Thaddeus Kosciusko, a native of Poland and a professional soldier trained in the classic European style of warfare, served as Greene's chief engineering officer. Kosciusko advised Greene to focus on reducing the strongest point of the loyalist defenses, the star fort. This in itself wasn't necessarily a bad plan. The Patriots compromised it, however, by digging their first trench line only seventy yards from the British earthwork and placing a three-gun battery only 130 yards away.

Colonel Cruger must have had a hard time keeping a straight face as he watched the American blunder. While the Patriots dug their trench in the sun-baked clay, Cruger built a firing platform inside the fort. On May 23 three cannon mounted on the platform began to fire merrily away at the American artillery and the men in the trench. The cannonfire was supported by sharpshooters on the platform, with the expected results. The thirty Tories who rushed out of the fort and charged the patriot work party were followed by a group of slaves. While the Tories bayoneted anyone who hadn't scurried back to the American lines, the slaves gathered up the American's entrenching tools and carried them off. General Greene's siege of Ninety Six was off to a bad start.

The Patriots pulled back to a more conventional distance and began again, but the Loyalists kept up a heavy fire on the workers. To counter this, the Americans built a Maham Tower, a 40-foot-high structure from which they could fire down into the fort. Colonel Cruger tried to burn the tower by firing hotshot at it, but between the lack of proper furnaces within the village to get the iron red-hot and the fact that the tower was constructed with green logs, that effort didn't work. Undaunted, Cruger simply piled sandbags on top of the fort's walls, raising them three feet and providing added protection for his sharpshooters.

With his tower complete, Greene sent a demand for surrender to Cruger, stating that further resistance would be folly. Since the garrison had, up to that point, suffered a total of one officer killed and eight men wounded, Cruger figured he could keep up the folly a while longer.

Next, Greene had his men fire flaming arrows into the fort in an attempt to ignite the roofs and burn the Loyalists out. Cruger stripped the shingles off all the rooftops so there would be nothing to ignite.

Despite these failures on the part of the attackers, the situation was becoming quite uncomfortable for the defenders of Ninety Six. By this time the Loyalists' fresh rations were gone, and they were relying on their salted reserves. To make matters worse, their water supply was in jeopardy.

Greene had become so focused on reducing the star fort itself that he had overlooked the true Achilles' heel of the Ninety Six garrison. The only source of water for the village was a stream to the west of the stockade and outside its protection. As anyone who has spent time in the interior of South Carolina during the summer can tell you, the region would make a great training ground for Satan's minions. The heat and humidity of the fast-approaching summer was taking its toll on the defenders. Water was critical to their ability to hold out.

Cruger hadn't overlooked this weakness in the position's defenses. A small stockade fort had been built by the stream, and a covered trench ran from the fort to the stockade walls of the village. No doubt grateful that Greene had thus far overlooked this weakness, Cruger had to know that it wouldn't escape the Patriots' attention forever, so he had his men dig a well inside the fort. Unfortunately they did not strike water.

On June 8, after his success in Augusta, Georgia, Lieutenant Colonel Henry ("Light-Horse Harry") Lee arrived with his legion to reinforce the Patriots. Lee was given the task of taking the little fort that protected the stream and cutting off the water supply. Although he never actually took the fort, he constructed trenches so close to it that the only way the Loyalists could get water was to send out slaves with jugs under the cover of darkness to bring in what little they could.

As time passed, the situation within the stockade and the star fort grew more desperate. Word arrived on June 12 that Lord Rawdon, British commander of the Carolinas, had left Charleston with a force of 2,000 British regulars to relieve the garrison. Time was running out for Nathaniel Greene. He decided to take Ninety Six by direct assault—if he could. The battle that Greene couldn't lose was in danger of slipping away.

The attack began the morning of June 18. Greene laid down a heavy artillery bombardment in hopes of softening up the position for his ground troops. At noon, the Patriots started forward.

One of the defensive features of the star fort was a 12-foot-deep trench outside the walls. To counter this, the Patriots sent forward men to fill a section of the trench with brush and logs, thus creating a walkway for the assaulting force to cross. Close on the heels of the first troops came men armed with long poles tipped with iron hooks to pull down the sandbags so the sharpshooters in the tower could drive the defenders back from the walls. The Patriots expected to break through and claim Ninety Six as their own.

For a few brief minutes, it seemed as if the plan would work, yet as the Patriots began to pull down the sandbags, the Tories sent two groups of thirty men each out of the rear of the fort. Unseen, they circled around inside the protective trench and hit the Patriots on both flanks. A brief but bloody hand-to-hand struggle resulted, and the Patriots were driven back.

That same day Greene learned that Lord Rawdon was less than thirty miles away. Knowing he would soon be outnumbered almost two to one, he had no choice but to break off the siege and retreat. Against all odds, Ninety Six was still in British hands. Nathaniel Greene had lost another battle.

Nevertheless, Greene's objective was reached—the British soon abandoned Ninety Six for the safety of Charleston. Although he hadn't taken the fort himself, Greene had the satisfaction of knowing another large part of South Carolina had been returned to the Patriots. The British would never again maintain a permanent garrison at Ninety Six—unless you count a few ghosts.

Merle McGee has been studying Ninety Six for a long time. A volunteer at the national park there, he's been tramping around the site since before it became a national park. There's not a great deal that Merle doesn't know about the place—except how to explain what happened to him early one evening back in the late seventies.

"I was walking along an old county access road, and I had one of the neighborhood dogs with me," Merle told me. "Back in those days, especially after a rain, you could walk along and find artifacts, bullets and the like, lying right on the surface, right along the road bed.

"The dog and I were the only ones around. It was raining pretty good that evening, coming down steady. We were walking from the star fort toward the jail site [inside the stockaded village] when, all of a sudden, the dog stopped. He stood there like he was frozen to the spot. The hair was standing up on his back, and his head was down, like he was staring at something down the road.

"Then I heard someone say, 'Company, halt.' That was it, just that command, two words. Heard it clear as a bell.

"I didn't think anything of it and went on toward the jail, expecting to find a reenactment unit drilling or something there, yet there wasn't a soul to be found. The archaeologists weren't there because of the weather, but I really expected to find some reenactors. Not only that, there weren't any footprints in the mud around the excavation site, which is where the voice had come from. As muddy as it was, as hard as it was raining—well, there should have been some footprints, but there weren't."

Mr. McGee isn't sure what it was he heard that day, he's just sure that he heard it. Another thing he is certain of is that his mind wasn't playing tricks on him. A retired military officer, he isn't given to flights of fancy. "People ask me all the time, 'was it a ghost?' I don't know. I just know I heard those two words. And it's the only time it ever happened; I've never heard anything there again."

There is more. A few years ago a reenactor left in the middle of a living history weekend, telling the park rangers in charge of the event that he couldn't spend another night in the park. He said he hadn't been able to get any sleep because of the voices.

The rangers said it really wasn't their responsibility, but if he would like, they would have a word with the rest of the group and ask them to turn in at a reasonable hour that evening.

"Oh, no, it wasn't any of the other guys," the man said. "I was camped over by the dry well, by myself." The reenactor looked uncomfortable and paused for a moment before continuing. "Besides," he said, "the voices were coming from all around and inside the well. Believe me, it wasn't any of the other guys, and I just don't think I want to stay here any longer."

Apparently there are also spirits there who had nothing to do with the battle. In the days before the war a trader named Robert Goudy and his family had a trading post at Ninety Six. While there is nothing left of the actual buildings, the site is marked in a stand of woods by an old cemetery that has forty or fifty gravesites. Two daughters of one of the rangers who has been at the park for a number of years used to enjoy horseback riding all through the park—until something happened one afternoon. Down near the woods they heard the sounds of children laughing and playing. They rode toward the cemetery, where the sounds originated, to investigate. Although they found no one there, the childish noises continued. They now refuse to go near that section of the park.

The ghostly children were reported by another person as well. About three years after the girls' experience, Merle McGee, who was leading a walking tour of the site, was asked why children were allowed to play in the old cemetery. One of the gentlemen in the group told him that he had been walking around the park earlier and had heard them.

"I followed the sound down to the cemetery and was going to ask them to stop, to tell them that it really wasn't a proper place for them to be playing," he said. "But when I got there, they weren't around. I don't know where they got to, but someone should look in to it."

Ninety Six National Historic Site is easily reached from either Columbia or Greenville, South Carolina. If you're travelling through that part of the state, it's well worth your time to stop by and visit the park. You just might want to make sure that if you have children, don't let them join in the first game they see—or hear.

Write to Ninety Six National Historic Site, P.O. Box 496, Ninety Six, South Carolina 29666-0496, or call (864) 543-4068.

The Haunts of Fort Pulaski

FORT PULASKI NATIONAL MONUMENT
SAVANNAH, GEORGIA

Without question one of the most beautiful cities in the United
States, if not the world, is Savannah, Georgia. The fact that
Sherman's army was so charmed by it that they did no looting nor
burning there speaks volumes of the grace that is a living, physical
presence felt by all. There are, however, those who claim to sense a
different type of presence amid the grid of park-studded streets.
Savannah is said to have one of the largest populations of spirits in
the country.

Among the many haunted sites near Savannah, one of the best
known is Fort Pulaski. Recorded sightings at that bastion on the
Savannah River date back to the 1940s. The ghostly encounters run
the gamut from a phantom garrison manning the parapets to
footsteps that follow visitors and sentries who refuse to leave their
posts to aid visitors. This story involves a sighting that took place a
few years ago by a group of reenactors.

Knowing that it was vital to the safety of the prosperous seaport,
Georgia state troops had seized Fort Pulaski even before the state
seceded from the Union. Built on Cockspur Island, the fort, named

for Revolutionary War hero Casimir Pulaski, guarded the approach up the Savannah River from the Atlantic to the city. Work began in 1829 and was completed eighteen years later. Among the U.S. army engineers who built the brick fort was a young lieutenant named Robert E. Lee.

Fort Pulaski was considered to be the epitome of coastal fortifications when it was completed, but by the time war broke out, the advances in weaponry, especially long-range artillery, had made brick forts all but obsolete. Unfortunately for the militia who so confidently took over Pulaski in January 1861, that was but one of the many lessons the young Confederacy had yet to learn.

As winter gave way to spring in 1862, the federal blockade tightened up along the East Coast. An amphibious force under General Ambrose Burnside had landed in North Carolina, and Charleston was preparing for siege. In Savannah the citizens knew that they would be next. Let the Yankees try, they said confidently. Fort Pulaski will protect us from all harm.

The problem was, Pulaski really couldn't even protect itself. In February 1862, the Federals began constructing a battery on Tybee Island, some one to two miles from Pulaski's walls. They brought in thirty-six guns, including five 30-pounder Parrotts and five converted long-range smoothbores. Inside the fort Colonel Charles H. Olmstead and his garrison of about 400 men watched the Yankee batteries take position. Watching was really all they could do; they didn't have the manpower to assault the federal position, and the fort's guns couldn't reach the enemy's batteries. It would come down to a test of which was stronger, the Yankees' rifled guns or the fort.

By early April the Federals had everything in place. General David Hunter, commander of the union forces, sent a demand for the unconditional surrender of the fort, which Col. Olmstead refused.

At 8:15 a.m. on April 10, when the federal batteries opened fire, the Confederates could do no more than hunker down. The solid brick fort might have been able to withstand the huffing and puffing of a Yankee wolf, but well-placed rifled cannon fire were another story. In about five hours a hole had been knocked into the fort's southeastern wall. Having made their first breach, the Federals, smelling blood, increased their fire. By nightfall a good portion of the wall had been reduced to rubble.

Inside the fort Olmstead and his men were shell-shocked, figuratively and literally. Considering the amount of shells hurled at the fort, it was remarkable that no one was killed, but even so, the psychological damage of seeing their once-invincible bastion reduced to rubble and dust was devastating.

As the shelling continued through the morning of the 11th, Olmstead contemplated what to do. Then, when shells began to land around the fort's magazine, the colonel knew he no longer had a choice; one well-placed round would reduce Fort Pulaski and everyone inside it to a fireworks display the likes of which Savannah had never seen. At 2 p.m. the flag was lowered, and Olmstead surrendered the fort. Even though he would be vilified in many homes for surrendering with only one man killed, he knew he had done his duty as a soldier. With no possible hope of victory, holding out further, until more men died, would have been suicide, not war.

Quite a few of the defenders of Fort Pulaski were from Savannah and the surrounding area. As they marched out of the fort, more than likely a number of them felt shame for having let down their families and neighbors. Perhaps it is a quest for redemption that keeps a few of their spirits standing watch over the fort today. For the ghost encountered by the reenactors from North Carolina late one afternoon, that seemed to be the case.

Much of the movie *Glory*, which tells the story of the assault of the 54th Massachusetts on Fort Wagner, was filmed around Savannah and nearby Amelia Island. Quite a few reenactors were involved in the filming, making the movie one of the most historically accurate in terms of uniforms, equipage and combat scenes. Apparently the reenactors were authentic enough in their appearance to have fooled the ghost.

The group—nine of them—were visiting Fort Pulaski on their way to take part in the filming. As they walked around its outside walls and admired the massive construction, they noticed a young man in the uniform of a confederate lieutenant. A couple of the reenactors gave him a comradely nod.

"Halt," said the young officer. His voice had a soft Savannah accent. "Don't you men salute a superior officer when you see one?"

He took a few steps toward them. A couple of the reenactors shrugged, and a few threw a sloppy salute. One didn't feel like playing along. "Who does that damned pup think he is?" he asked. "We ain't on the set yet!"

The lieutenant reacted harshly. "Sir, I don't know to what you are referring, and frankly don't care. Your insolence, however, will be noted and not tolerated. Now, fall in! Colonel Olmstead has recalled all work parties. The Yankee attack is imminent."

The group decided to play along. They thought perhaps there were people watching from the fort, and he wanted to put on a show. They formed up into a column and awaited the next order. "Attention! About face!" The group stiffened, wheeled about, and waited for the anticipated "forward march."

And they waited. And they waited. Finally, one of them glanced back over his shoulder and exclaimed, "What the—? Where did that fella go?" Where the aggressive young lieutenant had stood just seconds before, there was only a patch of sawgrass gently swaying in the light afternoon breeze.

"We searched all around the place," one of the reenactors told me. "Never found any trace of him. We kept an eye out around the movie set, too. Never saw him there, either. Hard as it is to believe, we've all pretty much accepted he was a ghost." He laughed. "If he wasn't, we'd sure like to hear from him—that was one good-looking uniform he had on!"

Contact Fort Pulaski National Monument at P.O. Box 30757, Savannah, Georgia 31410, or call (912) 786-5787.

Acknowledgements

It has always struck me as odd that many authors express appreciation to their spouse "last, but not least." The simple fact is, without that support, no married writer would ever complete a manuscript. I would, therefore, like to acknowledge my lovely wife Jill first and foremost. Her love, kindness, support, encouragement, good nature and advice made this book possible. Without her, I couldn't have gone beyond the first couple of pages.

Second, I would like to thank my publisher and editor, Kathie Tennery, and co-editor, Tracey Barger, of Rockbridge Publishing Company. It's always a pleasure to work with these two ladies, and the simple fact that they've managed to make my writing look good enough for public consumption speaks volumes about their talent.

When I start thinking of everyone who played a role in bringing these stories together, I'm reminded of the old Hollywood spectaculars with the "cast of thousands." It would take another book the size of this one to properly recognize each one for all that they've done, so I won't even try.

Everyone mentioned was instrumental in his or her own way, and I thank you all: Ted Alexander, Jim Anderson, Harold Barnett, Morris Bass, Gail Becker, Jimmy Blankenship, Fred Burgess, Roger Carpenter, David Farrow, Mike Fraering, John Golden, Rod Gragg,

Will Greene, Rick Hatcher, Dawn Haun, Durham Hunt, Chuck Johnson, Mike Jones, Henry Kidd, Telley Kirkland, Dr. Richard Kobetz, Gary Kross, Margaret Lee, Bob Mallin, Merle McGee, Beth McGuire, Kaye McNulty, Dr. William McNulty, David Melton, Dr. Bobby G. Moss, Matthew Murdzak, Greg Potts, Rick Reeves, Chris Revels, Farrell Saunders, Bill Scaife, Eddie Shuman, Kenneth Stiles, Dr. Gary Stone, Lark Thornton, the late Warren Wilkinson, Manning Williams, Chuck Winchester, and Terry Winschel.

And last, but certainly not least, thank you to the very special few who helped to bring these stories alive, yet who chose to remain anonymous.

SELECT BIBLIOGRAPHY

Bailey, Ronald H. *The Bloodiest Day: The Battle of Antietam*. Richmond: Time-Life Books, 1984.

Barrett, John G. *The Civil War in North Carolina*. Chapel Hill, N.C.: Univ. of North Carolina Press, 1963.

Bradley, Mark L. *Last Stand in the Carolinas: The Battle of Bentonville*. Campbell, Calif.: Savas-Woodbury Publishers, 1996.

"Brandywine Battlefield Cultural Resources Management Study." Files of Brandywine Battlefield National Historic Landmark, 1989.

Faust, Patricia L., ed. *Historical Times Illustrated Encyclopedia of the Civil War*. New York: Harper & Row Publishers, Inc., 1986.

Foote, Shelby. *The Civil War: A Narrative, Vols. I-III*. New York: Random House, 1958.

Freeman, Douglas S. *Lee's Lieutenants: A Study in Command, Vols. I-III*. New York: Charles Scribner's Sons, 1942.

Gragg, Rod. *Confederate Goliath: The Battle of Fort Fisher*. New York: Harper-Collins Publishers, 1991.

Guttman, John. "'Old Abe' Goes to War," *America's Civil War*. November 1990.

Hughes, Nathaniel Cheairs, Jr. *Bentonville: The Final Battle of Sherman and Johnston*. Chapel Hill, N.C.: Univ. of North Carolina Press, 1996.

Joslyn, Mauriel P. *Charlotte's Boys: Civil War Letters of the Branch Family of Savannah*. Berryville, Va.: Rockbridge Publishing Co., 1996.

Korn, Jerry. *War on the Mississippi: Grant's Vicksburg Campaign*. Richmond: Time-Life Books, 1985.

Lee, Winkie. "Ghost Tales, History Mix at Bentonville Site," Raleigh *News and Observer*, 5 November 1990.

Lewis, Thomas A. *The Shenandoah in Flames: The Valley Campaign of 1864*. Richmond: Time-Life Books, 1987.

Lumpkin, Henry. *From Savannah to Yorktown*. New York: Paragon House, 1987.

Mahr, Theodore C. *The Battle of Cedar Creek: Showdown in the Shenandoah, October 1-30, 1864*. Lynchburg, Va.: H. E. Howard, Inc., 1992.

Messick, Hank. *Kings Mountain*. Boston: Little-Brown, 1976.

Pancake, John. *This Destructive War: The British Campaign in the Carolinas, 1780-1782*. Tuscaloosa, Ala.: Univ. of Alabama Press, 1985.

Priest, John Michael. *Antietam: The Soldier's Battle*. Shippensburg, Pa.: White Mane Publ. Co., 1989.

Savas, Theodore P. and David A. Woodbury, eds. *The Campaign for Atlanta and Sherman's March to the Sea: Essays on the American Civil War, Vols. I & II*. Campbell, Calif.: Savas-Woodbury Publishers, 1994.

Sears, Stephen W. *Landscape Turned Red: The Battle of Antietam*. New Haven, Conn.: Ticknor & Fields, 1983.

Symmes, Rev. Frank R. *History of the Old Tennent Church*. Cranbury, N.J.: George W. Burroughs, Printer, 1901.

Trotter, William R. *Ironclads & Columbiads: The Civil War in North Carolina, Vol. III, The Coast*. Greensboro, N.C.: Signal Research, Inc., 1989.

Trudeau, Noah A. *The Last Citadel: Petersburg, Virginia, June 1864-April 1865*. Boston: Little-Brown, 1976.

Trussell, John B.B., Jr. *The Battle of Brandywine*. Harrisburg: Commonwealth of Pennsylvania, 1988.

Wert, Jeffry A. *From Winchester to Cedar Creek: The Shenandoah Valley Campaign 1864*. New York: Simon & Schuster, 1987.

Wood, W. J. *Battles of the Revolutionary War 1775-1781*. Chapel Hill, N.C.: Algonquin Books, 1990.

Yearns, W. Buck, and John G. Barrett. *North Carolina Civil War Documentary*. Chapel Hill, N.C.: Univ. of North Carolina Press, 1980.

INDEX

R
Ramseur, Stephen Dodson 41-44
Rawdon, Lord 96
Reilly, James 48
Richardson, Israel 3
Rodes, Robert 2
Rommel, Erwin 12, 14
Rosser, Thomas 41
S
Savannah, Georgia 100
Schofield, John 90
Sevier, John 66, 69, 71-72
Sharpsburg, Maryland 2
Shelby, Isaac 69, 71-72
Sherfy, John 7
Sheridan, Philip 20-22, 39-41
Sherman, William 75, 78, 81-82,
    88-90
Shields, James 30
Sickles, Daniel 7
Slocum, Henry 76-78
Soldier's Rest 29
Springdale 33
Stewart, A.P. 76, 78
Stiles, Kenneth 20
Stonewall Brigade 31
Stonewall Cemetery 11-12, 14-15,
    22
T
Tarleton, Banastre 68
Taylor, Richard 61
Terry, Alfred 47
Toney, Jill 24-27
Trostle, Abraham 7
U
U.S. Military Academy 39
U.S. National Park Service 9

V
Vaughan, Alfred 90
Vicksburg Nat'l Military Park 50-64
Vicksburg, Mississippi 62
von Knyphausen, Wilhelm 17-18,
    35
W
Washington, George 16-18, 36-37
Washington, Mrs. 22, 31
Waverly Farm 20, 22-23
Waxhaws, North Carolina 67-68
Wayne, Anthony 16-19, 36
Wheeler, Joseph 76
Whiting, William 45, 47-48
Williams, Alpheus 77-78
Williams, Philip 13
Wilmington, North Carolina 45, 46
Wilson, James H. 21
Winchester, Virginia 29
Wood, Thomas 83-84

ABOUT THE AUTHOR

B. Keith Toney, a native of Marion, North Carolina, in the western North Carolina mountains, is a life-long student of American history. He has served as a Licensed Battlefield Guide at Gettysburg National Military Park since 1990.

The author of *Gettysburg: Tours and Tales with a Battlefield Guide*, a collection of humorous and informative short stories about the Gettysburg battlefield, he also authored the premiere issue of Cowles History Group's *Civil War Art* magazine, which featured the "Three Days of Gettysburg." He has had several articles published in local and regional publications and is one of the featured book review editors for *America's Civil War* magazine.

He lives in Winchester, Virginia, with his wife, Jill, and their children, Billy and Katie.

Some Other Fine Books on the Civil War, Ghosts, Folklore, and Touring the South. Call for FREE CATALOG.

Rockbridge Publishing Company
an imprint of Howell Press, Inc.
1147 River Road, Suite 2 • Charlottesville, Va 22901
Order Line: (800) 868-4512 • Information: (804) 977-4006
e-mail: howellpres@aol.com

Banshees, Bugles and Belles: True Ghost Stories of Georgia, Barbara Duffey. Includes unretouched photos of "live" spirits. $15 paperback.

Charlotte's Boys: CW Letters of the Branch Family of Savannah, Mauriel P. Joslyn. Saga begins before Fort Sumter, ends after Appomattox. $32 hardcover.

The Confederacy's Forgotten Son: MG James L. Kemper, CSA, Harold R. Woodward, Jr. "A solid biography of this neglected Confederate." $22 hardcover.

Defender of the Valley: BG John D. Imboden, CSA, Harold R. Woodward, Jr. The only full biography on the cavalry leader of the Valley. $25 hardcover.

The Dulanys of Welbourne: A Family in Mosby's Confederacy, Margaret A. Vogtsberger. Powerful letters chronicle the chaotic and suspenseful day-to-day-life of a prominent family. $32 hardcover.

Jack Burd's Civil War Source Book 1997, Jack Burd. Complete guide to people, places, events & products. $10 paperback.

Maryland: The South's First Casualty, Bart Rhett Talbert. A wake-up call to those who think she was a northern state. $25 hardcover.

Prince of Edisto: BG Micah Jenkins, CSA, James Swisher. A Conferate hero who did not live to pen his memoirs. $25 hardcover.

Season of Fire: The Confederate Strike on Washington, Joseph Judge. Military Book Club feature selection. $30 hardcover.

Shenandoah Voices: Folklore, Legends and Traditions of the Valley, John L. Heatwole. Award-winning story collection. $25 hardcover.

In Virginia, please add 4.5% sales tax. Shipping is $3.50 for the first title, $.75 each add'l title to the same address. MasterCard, VISA, Amex, and Discover accepted.